Many Points Make a Point

Data and Graphs

STUDENT BOOK

TERC

Mary Jane Schmitt, Myriam Steinback,
Tricia Donovan, and Martha Merson

Key Curriculum Press
Innovators in Mathematics Education

TERC
2067 Massachusetts Avenue
Cambridge, Massachusetts 02140

Key College Publishing and Key Curriculum Press:
Development Editor: Elizabeth McCue
Production Director: McKinley Williams
Production Project Managers: Beth Masse, Ken Wischmeyer
Consultant: Donna Curry
Text Designer: Laura Murray Productions
Proofreader: Erin Milnes
Photo Researcher: Laura Murray Productions
Art and Design Coordinator: Kavitha Becker
Cover and Logo Design: Kavitha Becker, Marilyn Perry
Cover Photo Credit: CREATAS/Corbis
Printer: Alonzo

Editorial Director: Richard J. Bonacci
Vice President/General Manager: Mike Simpson
Publisher: Steven Rasmussen

EMPower Research and Development Team
Principal Investigator: Myriam Steinback
Co-Principal Investigator: Mary Jane Schmitt
Research Associate: Martha Merson
Curriculum Developer: Tricia Donovan

Contributing Authors
Donna Curry
Marlene Kliman

Technical Team
Graphic Designer and Project Assistant: Juania Ashley
Production and Design Coordinator: Valerie Martin
Copyeditor: Jill Pellarin

Evaluation Team
Brett Consulting Group:
Belle Brett
Marilyn Matzko

EMPower™ was developed at TERC in Cambridge, Massachusetts. This material is based upon work supported by the National Science Foundation under award number ESI-9911410. Any opinions, findings, and conclusions or recommendations expressed in this publication are those of the authors and do not necessarily reflect the views of the National Science Foundation.

TERC is a not-for-profit education research and development organization dedicated to improving mathematics, science, and technology teaching and learning.

Key Curriculum Press
1150 65th Street
Emeryville, CA 94608
510-595-7000
editorial@keycollege.com
www.keypress.com

Printed in the United States of America
10 9 8 7 6 5 4 3 08 07

ISBN 1-55953-720-5

Contents

Introduction

Welcome to EMPower

Students using the EMPower books often find that EMPower's approach to mathematics is different from the approach found in other math books. For some students, it is new to talk about mathematics and to work on math in pairs or groups. The math in the EMPower books will help you connect the math you use in everyday life to the math you learn in your coursel.

We asked some students what they thought about EMPower's approach. We thought we would share some of their thoughts with you to help you know what to expect.

"It's more hands-on."

"More interesting."

"I use it in my life."

"We learn to work as a team."

"Our answers come from each other… [then] we work it out ourselves."

"Real-life examples like shopping and money are good."

"The lessons are interesting."

"I can help my children with their homework."

"It makes my brain work."

"Math is fun."

EMPower's goal is to make you think and to give you puzzles you will want to solve. Work hard. Work smart. Think deeply. Ask why.

Using This Book

This book is organized by lessons. Each lesson has the same format.

- The first page explains the lesson and states the purpose of the activity. Look for a question to keep in mind as you work.
- The activity page comes next. You will work on the activities in class, sometimes with a partner or in a group.
- Look for shaded boxes with additional information and ideas to help you get started if you become stuck.

- Practice pages follow the activities. These practices will make sense to you after you have done the activity. The three types of practice pages are

  Practice: provides another chance to see the math from the activity and to use new skills.

  Extension: presents a challenge with a more difficult problem or a new but related math idea.

  Test Practice: asks a number of multiple-choice questions and one open-ended question.

In the *Appendices* at the end of the book, there is space for you to keep track of what you have learned and to record your thoughts about how you can use the information.

- Use notes, definitions, and drawings to help you remember new words in *Vocabulary*, pages 143–45.
- Answer the *Reflections* questions after each lesson, pages 146–53.

Check *Sources and Resources*, pages 156–57, for books and Internet sites related to the unit.

Tips for Success

Where do I begin?

Many people do not know where to begin when they look at their math assignments. If this happens to you, first try to organize your information.

Much of this unit is about data or information and how to show it.

Ask yourself:

> *What organization makes sense for these data? Can I use a frequency graph, a bar graph, or a circle graph? What could I learn from each?*

Another part of getting organized is figuring out what skills are required.

Ask yourself:

> *What do I already know? What do I need to find out?*

Write down what you already know.

I cannot do it. It seems too hard.

Make the numbers smaller. Deal with just a little bit of data at a time. Cross out information or data that you do not need.

Ask yourself:

> *Is there information in this problem that I do not need?*
>
> *Have I ever seen something like this before? What did I do then?*

You can always look back at another lesson for ideas.

Am I done?

Don't walk away yet. Check your answers to make sure they make sense.

Ask yourself:

Did I include all the data that I should have?

Does the graph I created seem reasonable? Does the graph represent the data I used? Do the conclusions I am drawing from the graph seem logical?

Check your math with a calculator. Ask others whether your work makes sense to them.

Opening the Unit: Many Points Make a Point

What information does the graph communicate to you?

Graphs and charts are ways to show information without a lot of words. On the job, at home, at the health clinic, or in test situations, you may be expected to understand **graphs** and make decisions based on their information. When you are able to organize the many points of a data set into a graph that tells a story, you will be able to make your own point more effectively.

By the end of this unit, you will have become familiar with how graphs are created, as well as how to interpret them. This understanding will help you look critically at graphs before making decisions and predictions based on them.

Activity 1: Making a Mind Map

Make a Mind Map using words, numbers, pictures, or ideas that come to mind when you think of *data and graphs.*

DATA and GRAPHS

Activity 2: Initial Assessment

Complete *Task 1, Decisions* on the *Initial Assessment*. For *Tasks 2* and *3*, your teacher will give you some problems and ask you to check off how you feel about your ability to solve each problem:

___ Can do ____ Don't know how ____ Not sure

Have you ever noticed that every new place you work has its own words or specialized vocabulary? This is true of topics in math too. In every lesson you will be introduced to some specialized vocabulary. Do not worry if you see words in the problems that you do not recognize. You can write some words down and look them up later or learn as you go.

Activity 3: Sorting Graphs

Sort the graphs in your packet into groups that make sense to you.

1. How did you sort the graphs?

2. How are the graphs in each pile alike?

3. How are the graphs in each pile different?

Practice: The Graph I Chose

The graph that interests me is ______________________________.

Staple or tape the graph to this page.

1. What about the graph interests you? Why?

2. What did you learn from reading the graph?

Practice: Data Collection

Article of Clothing	Country

About My Data

What I noticed …

What surprised me …

What turned out as I expected …

Most of my clothes came from ______________________________.

Many Points Make a Point Unit Goals

- Collect, organize, and represent data.
- Make accurate statements about data using percents and fractions.
- Create and interpret frequency graphs, bar graphs, circle graphs, and line graphs.
- Make predictions, decisions, and recommendations from information presented in bar, line, and circle graphs.
- Use scale to change the story a graph tells. Interpret graphs with different scales.
- Use mean and median to describe a data set.

My Own Goals

LESSON **1**

Countries in Our Closets

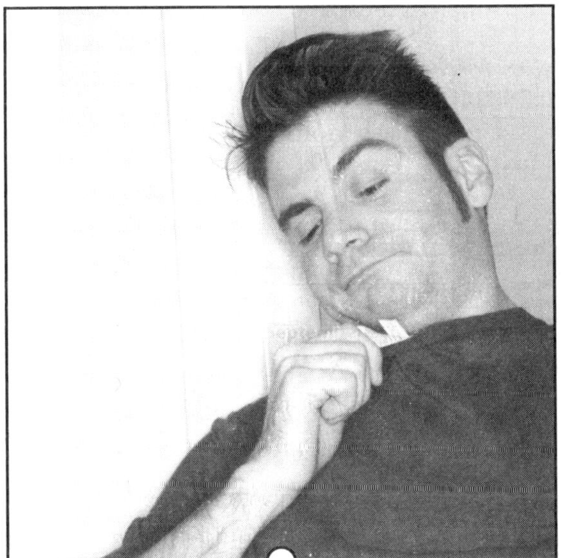

Where were your clothes made?

In a world where information is at our fingertips, it is important to be able to make sense of it. What does it tell us? Why do we care?

Begin with your own clothes. Where were they made? Find out! You will collect **data** by reading the labels on your clothes. You will organize that data, make statements about it, and note where most of your clothes were made.

You will then try organizing the data in a different way. How will placing the data in new groups change the story of the countries in your closet? You will compare your class data to data of other classes. Will the stories be the same?

On Your Own

I think the country in which most of my clothes were made is

____.

Look at the labels of at least eight items of clothing. Make a list to keep track of the information you are collecting. Research question: Where were your favorite clothes made?

Activity 1: Organizing the Data

Look at the data you collected about countries where your clothes were made.

Organize the data.

1. What strikes you about your data?

2. What is the **mode** for your data?

3. What is the mode for the class data?

Frequency Graphs

Create an easy-to-use **frequency graph** by making a line. Use equal-size x's and equal spacing for each **category**. Line up your x's or use graph paper so it is easy to note which category contains the most data items.

Some people can look at a frequency graph and make true statements by "eyeballing," or visually estimating, the size of each category. For example:

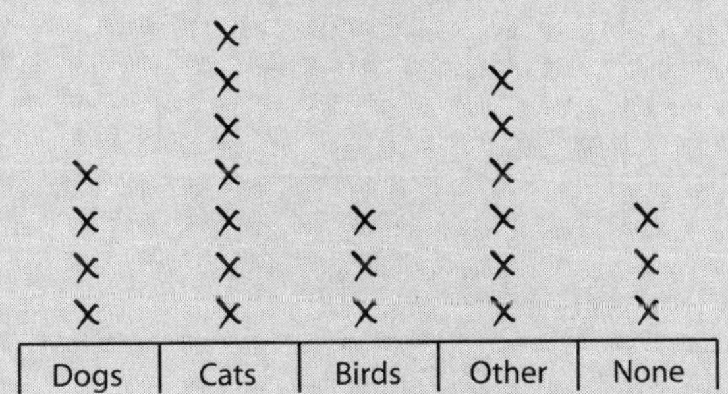

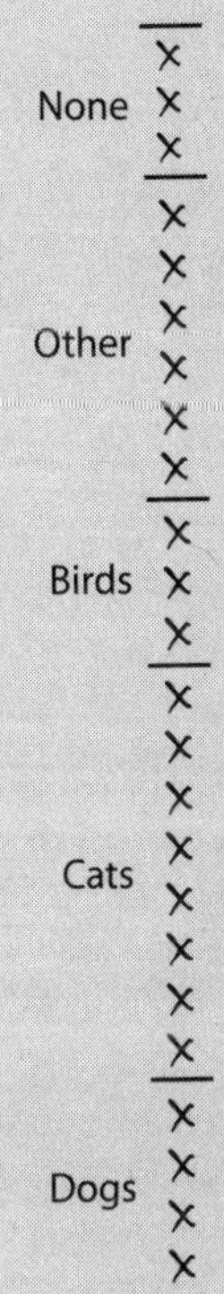

If you have a hard time visually estimating, try this: Count all the x's. Make one tall tower showing every x on the frequency graph. Compare each of the categories to the tower with all the data.

Does that category represent more than half, less than half, or exactly half of the data?

Compare two categories: Is one category more than half of the other?

Activity 2: Statements about Data

Use the data in the following frequency graph to fill in the blanks:

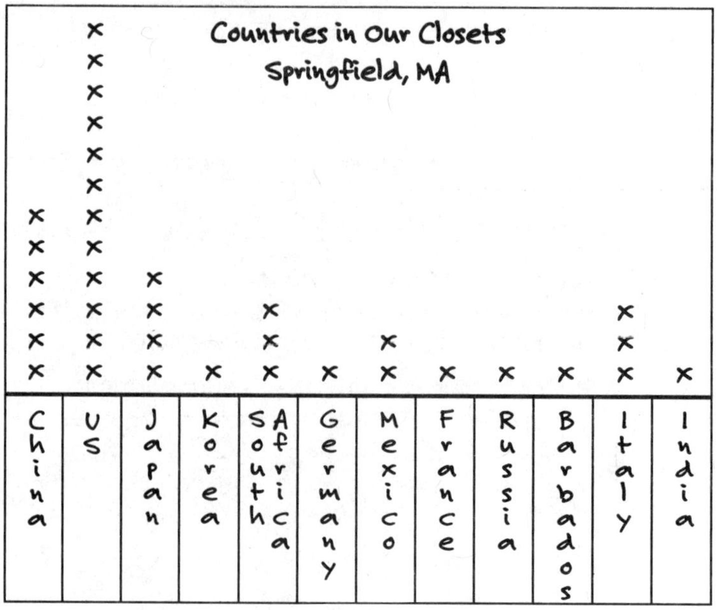

Use the following words to fill in the blanks:

half	six	United States	twice	three
one-fourth	four	one-third	Russia	China

1. There are ______________ times as many clothes from South Africa as from Barbados.
2. The number of clothes from Mexico is ______________ of the number of clothes from China.
3. ______________ as many clothes come from the United States as from China.
4. The clothes from Korea are ______________ as many as those from Japan.
5. ______________ countries have only one article of clothing.
6. ______________ of the clothes come from ______________ and ______________.
7. Japan has ______________ times as many clothes as Germany.

Activity 3: Changing the Categories

On grid paper, make a new frequency graph using the class data. Group the clothes by continent this time, instead of by country.

Frequency graphs have three components: a line, frequencies (marked with x's), and labels. When making your own graph, be sure to include all three parts.

1. What do you notice about these new groupings (continents)?

2. How is the story of this graph different from the story of the whole-class frequency graph by country?

3. What advantages do you see to this way of grouping? What disadvantages?

4. Make a numerical statement about the new organization of the data.

Practice: Clothes by Continent in Springfield, MA

Refer to the Springfield data on page 10.

1. Sort the data by continent and make a frequency graph on the graph paper below:

2. How do the data represented in the new graph compare to the data from the graph your class created?

3. Write one statement about the Springfield clothes frequency graph organized by continent.

Practice: Reporting Data 1

The race/ethnicity of 20 HIV/AIDS patients at a clinic in the United States is shown in the following frequency graph:

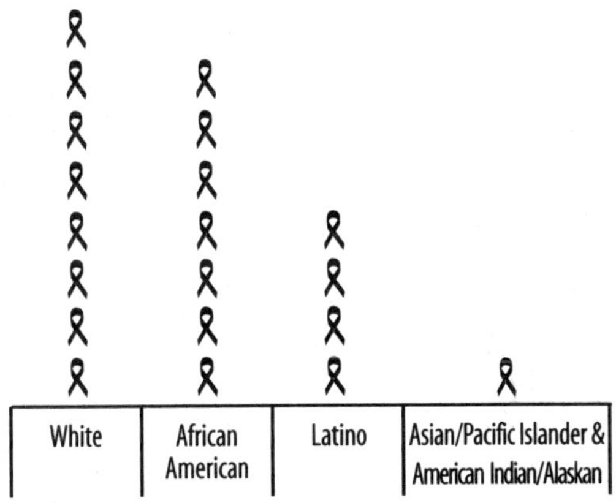

Source: Based on data from the AIDSHotline.org, 2003

1. Write a statement comparing two of the categories.

Ana reports the data from her clinic using only two categories: White and non-White.

2. Use grid paper to show what her frequency graph will look like.
3. How does using only two categories change the story of the HIV/AIDS data at her clinic?

4. Would you expect the data to be similar if the clinic were in your city, a city in Alaska, or a city in Florida?

5. Imagine a clinic in a city in your state. Show a frequency graph of 20 patients, categorized by race. Explain your thinking.

Practice: Reporting Data 2

The mayor wants to cut commuting time. He commissioned a survey to find out how long it takes people to get to work. The results were shown in five travel-time categories.

Regroup the data to show only three categories.

Travel Time to Work	Percent of Commuters	Number Based on 25 People
Less than 10 minutes	16%	4
10–19 minutes	32%	8
20–29 minutes	20%	5
30–44 minutes	20%	5
45 minutes or more	12%	3
Total	100%	25

Travel Time to Work	Percent of Commuters	Number Based on 25 People

Compare the two ways of organizing the information.

1. What is the travel-time category with the biggest percent of commuters?

   Five categories ___________ Three categories ___________

2. Which category has the smallest percent of people?

   Five categories ___________ Three categories ___________

3. How does regrouping the categories change your impression of people's travel time to work?

4. Which group would you recommend the mayor focus on if he starts a program to cut commuting time? Why?

Practice: Categorically Speaking

Sometimes we can organize categories into subgroups of other categories in order to better understand the data. For example, drug stores will often organize their aisles by category—skin care, beauty aids, and so on. Then the items in each of those aisles are also organized. This makes it easier to take inventory and place orders and for the customer to find products.

Can you think of other examples where information is categorized?

Use the chart below *or* create your own chart; draw a picture; make a list; or write about examples you see at home or at work. In the chart below, one example is given.

Location	**What Stuff or Information?**	**How Is It Organized?**
Drug store	Over-the-counter products they sell	Skin care Beauty aids Seasonal Stationery First aid Hair care

Extension: Taking Inventory

Find a drawer or closet filled with many things. Use a frequency graph to show the contents. Start with six categories. Then do another frequency graph to show the same items, but this time use three categories.

For example:

My Medicine Cabinet

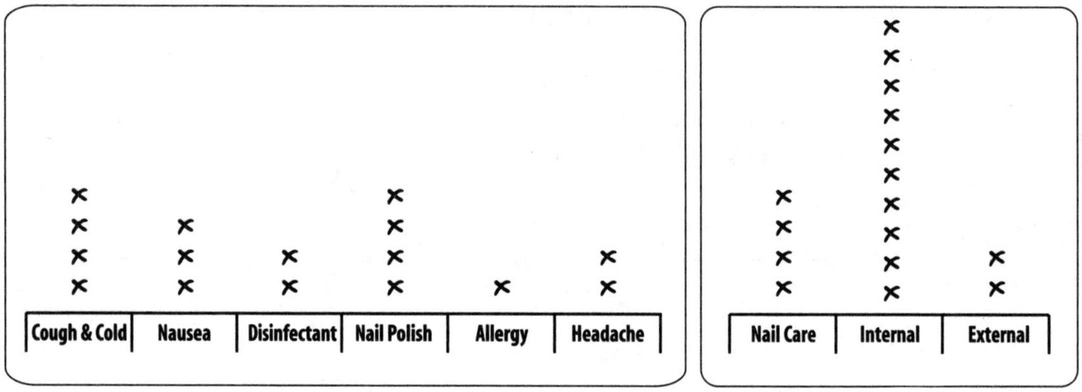

Test Practice

1. Freda worked at a printing press. She kept a tally of all the defects she found in the books she was processing. Based on the frequency graph she created, shown below, which of the following statements is true?

   (1) There were more defects related to colors than any other defect.

   (2) There were twice as many torn pages as there were warped spines.

   (3) There were more warped spines than colors that bled.

   (4) Half of all the defects were related to colors that bled.

   (5) Half of all the defects were related to pages that were torn.

Book Defects Frequency Graph

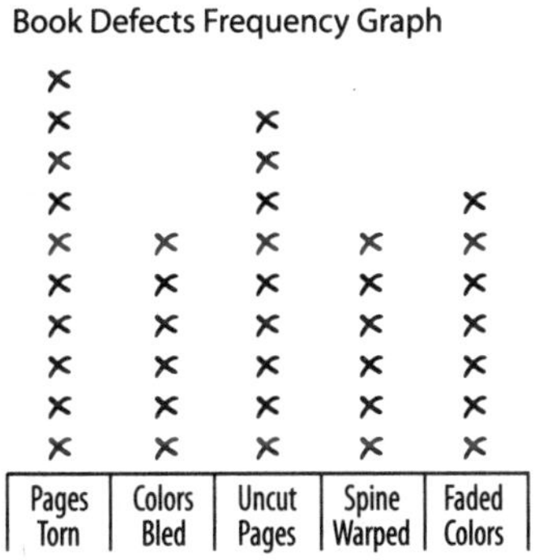

2. Tony, a tour guide, has been keeping a tally of visitors from different states. According to his tally, which of the following is *not* a true statement?

   (1) The fewest number of visitors came from Oregon.

   (2) There were as many visitors from Maine as there were from Georgia.

   (3) There were as many visitors from Georgia as there were from Oregon and Texas.

   (4) There were twice as many visitors from Florida as there were from Rhode Island.

   (5) There were twice as many visitors from Idaho as there were from Maine.

U.S. Tourist Frequency Graph

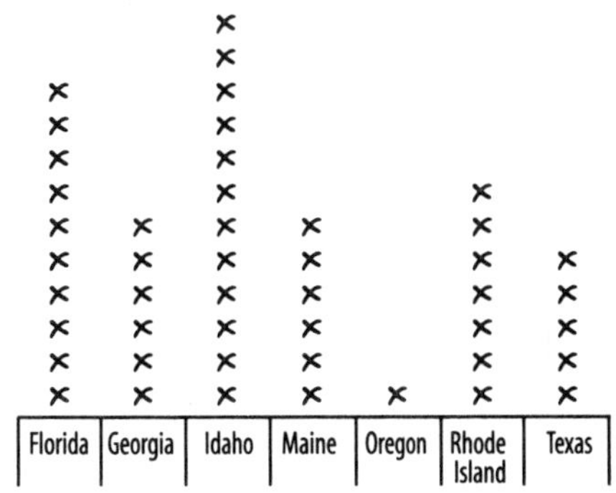

3. Clara is paid a commission on each of the large electronics devices that she sells. She tallied the different items she sold for the month. Based on her tally, what can she tell her boss about her sales?

   (1) She sold twice as many DVD players as she did TVs.

   (2) She sold twice as many DVD players as she did computers.

   (3) She sold more DVD players than she did TVs and computers combined.

   (4) She sold more TVs and VCRs than she did stereos and DVD players combined.

   (5) She sold half as many TVs as she did stereos.

Home Media Frequency Graph

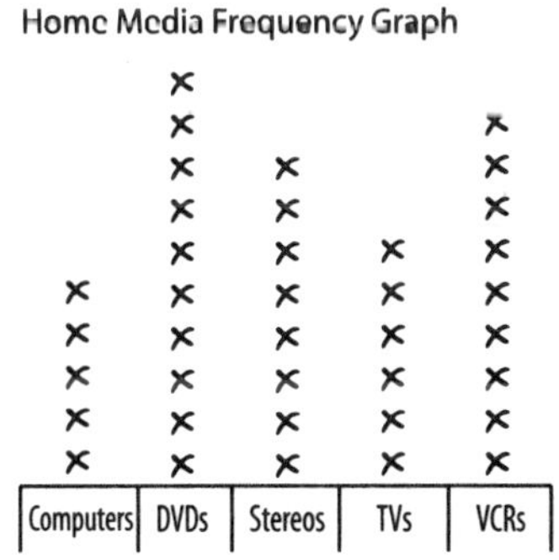

4. Bronson, a forest ranger in the Green Mountains, kept track of the different animals that were reportedly seen in one of the campgrounds during the month of May. Based on his tally, which of the following statements could he tell the media?

   (1) There were twice as many wolves reportedly seen as bears.

   (2) Half of all the reported sightings were wolves.

   (3) There were more bears than wolves reportedly seen.

   (4) There were twice as many moose reportedly seen than there were black bears.

   (5) One-quarter of all reported sightings were brown bears.

North American Wildlife Frequency Graph

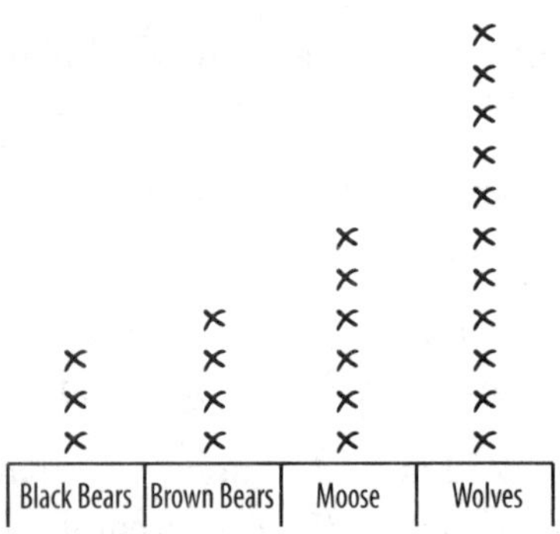

5. According to Global Exchange, some workers in China who make clothing for Disney are paid as little as $0.16 per hour. At this wage, what amount would a worker make for a 40-hour workweek?

   (1) $64.00

   (2) $6.40

   (3) $6.00

   (4) $80.00

   (5) $0.60

6. In 2003 the U.S. Department of Labor (DOL) issued new regulations for overtime pay. The DOL estimated that under the new regulations 1.3 million low-wage workers would become eligible for overtime pay, unless their wages were raised to $425 per week. The DOL estimated that 24.8 percent of those workers were Hispanic and 16.6 percent were African American. What percent were neither Hispanic nor African American?

LESSON **2**

Most of Us Eat...

What foods do you eat most often?

Who cares about what people living in the United States eat? Think about the people who grow, raise, advertise, package, label, and sell food. Add to them the people in healthcare who give advice on wellness.

To stay current, all of these people need to know what children and adults in the United States eat. How do they find out? In this lesson, you will get a taste of what it means to collect information, organize it, and learn from it. Finding the information is only part of the challenge. People who can take scattered bits of information and organize them can make decisions and influence others.

Activity 1: Frequently Eaten Foods

Write each food name on its own index card. Arrange and rearrange the information into groups that have something in common. For example, one way would be to group the items into raw and cooked foods. You will have a chance to think of other categories.

Before you begin, choose one person from your group to record information. Also be sure that everyone in your group gets a turn.

Steps:

1. Place the cards in two, three, four, or five categories, based on what they have in common.
2. Name each category and write down the number of cards you put in that category.
3. Allow group members to ask any questions they have.
4. Make any changes you want to the categories.
5. Have the recorder write on strips of paper the name of each category and the foods in it.
6. Once the group agrees on which categories to use, tape the cards with the names of the categories and the strips with the number of cards in each category onto the newsprint.

Make your own notes here:

Activity 2: Consistent Categories

In the four lists below, there is a problem with the categories. Circle the item that does not belong and explain why you think it does not fit with the others.

1. Parts of the hand

Fingers	Fingernails	Bones
Muscles	Joints	Elbow

2. Parts of the day

Morning	Evening
Afternoon	Early morning

3. Taxes

Sales tax	Food tax	Gas tax
Cigarette tax	Clothing tax	

4. At the shoe store

Sandals	Socks	Footwear	Sneakers
High heels	Flip-flops	Boots	

Write a category title for each list in the four problems below.

5. Title ________________

Carnivore	Herbivore
Omnivore	Insectivore

6. Title ________________

Earthquake	Flood	Mudslide	Fire
Tsunami	Drought	Blackout	Blizzard

7. Title ________________

Resume	Interview	Thank-you letter
Job application	Training	

8. Title ________________

Photosynthesis	Water	Soil	Sun
Roots	Leaves	Chlorophyll	

Activity 3: Describing the Data

Select one of the posters.

Write two statements, using benchmark fractions or percents, to describe the data on the poster.

Activity 4: Who to Ask?

1. A new restaurant is opening at the Magic Mall in Portland. The mall owner wants to know what types of food should be offered. Which of the following would be her best source of information?

   (1) Asking students in an adult education program in Cambridge

   (2) Surveying customers who are walking through Magic Mall

   (3) Quizzing children across the state about their favorite foods

2. A consumer group wants to know how much money Americans spend each year on dog food. Which of the following would be the best way to get a good sample of that information?

   (1) Randomly asking people who buy pets at pet stores in several malls across the country

   (2) Randomly asking people who buy dog food at various grocery and pet stores across the country

   (3) Randomly asking children who have dogs as pets

3. The president of a tool and die shop wants to find out whether his employees feel good about working for his company. Which of the following would be his best source of information?

   (1) Asking all of his supervisors

   (2) Asking his managers to complete an anonymous survey

   (3) Asking his employees to complete an anonymous survey

4. Mac, the vice-president of a large communications company, has heard about a new software program that could simplify his company's bookkeeping process. Before buying the new program, he wants to find out whether others think it would be useful. Which of the following would be his best source of information?

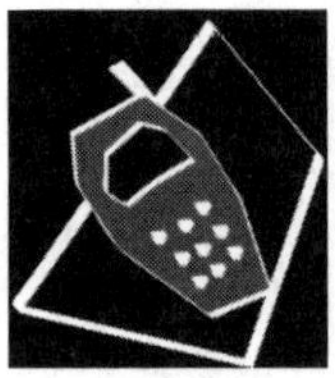

   (1) The employees who work in the bookkeeping department

   (2) The employees who are communications specialists

   (3) The managers and supervisors

Practice: Take a Sample

For each story below, think of a way the individual could choose a **sample** to get a good representation of data.

1. Freda, manager of an ice cream shop, wants to add a fun flavor—dill pickle sherbet—to the list of choices. Before creating this new flavor, she wants to know whether people will buy it. How could she find out this information?

   A good strategy for choosing a representative sample:

2. The Caddy Car Company wants to know whether their customers are happy with the service department. How could they find out this information?

A good strategy for choosing a representative sample:

3. Teachers in an adult education program want to know the reasons some students do not stay in the program long enough to complete their goals. How could they get this information?

A good strategy for choosing a representative sample:

Practice: Thirsty

A number of adults were asked what they drink most often. Here is what they said:

1. Organize the information into two, three, or four categories. You may need to rewrite the names of the drinks, each on its own Post-it® Note or piece of scrap paper.

2. Give each category a title.

3. Count the number of drinks in each category.

4. Write two statements about the data on drinks. Use a fraction or percent in each statement.

5. Finish these sentences:

   Most of the adults said…

   Only a few said…

   None said…

6. If the adults surveyed were students in your class, what type of drinks would you suggest bringing for a class party? Why?

In order to make statements, predictions, or decisions about categories of data, it is important to look at how *many* items are in each category and what the *total* number of items is. This chart might help you brainstorm statements that include fractions or percents.

Words	Percents	Near Fractions
All of us	100%	The whole or 1
Most of us	75–95%	$\frac{9}{12}$ or $\frac{3}{4}$
Half of us	50%	$\frac{6}{12}$ or $\frac{1}{2}$
Some of us	30–45%	$\frac{4}{12}$ or $\frac{1}{3}$
Only a few of us	10–25%	$\frac{3}{12}$ or $\frac{1}{4}$
None of us	0%	$\frac{0}{12}$ or 0

If you surveyed your classmates about their favorite drinks and most said "iced tea," the information could be helpful in shaping some decisions, but not others. If you were in charge of drinks for a class party, should you bring iced tea? It seems likely that most of your classmates would drink it. Should the nursing home nearby start serving iced tea instead of milk because 9 out of 10 students in your class said they liked iced tea? Probably not.

Practice: Ouch!

A number of adults wrote down the health issues their families had during the past winter:

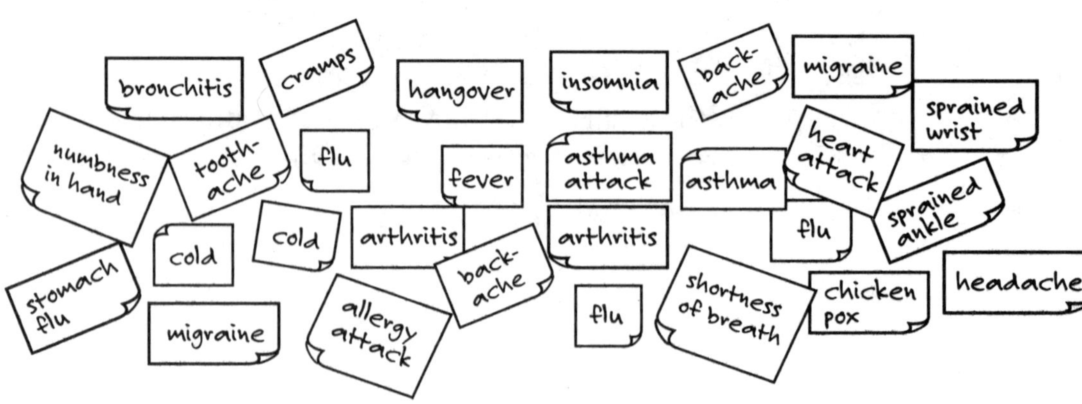

1. Organize the information in two ways:
   - Contagious and non-contagious
   - Possibly work-related, not work-related, and unclear

   (You may want to rewrite the conditions, each on its own Post-it Note or piece of scrap paper.)
2. Next follow these steps:
   a. Label the categories.
   b. Count the number of health-related issues in each category.
   c. Write two statements about the data using fractions or percents.

3. Finish these sentences:
   a. Most of the health issues were…

   b. None of the health issues were…

Extension: Friends and Family Drink Too

Plan to ask 10 other people—friends, family, neighbors—what their favorite drink is.

1. Before you ask, write down two predictions. What drinks do you think will be popular? Which category might make up more than half of all the answers?

2. Collect the data. Keep track of what you find out by placing each item on a separate card. Group the data.

3. Write three statements based on your data.

4. Are the data different from what you expected?

   Were there any surprises?

5. Now add your 10 cards to the data given in *Thirsty*, page 26.

6. You might have to create a new category based on the new information. How do your categories compare to the categories created by your classmates? What happens to the number of items in each category?

Extension: Data Collection

Collect data on the foods you eat in a week, keeping track with this chart:

Foods I Eat in a Week
(no drinks)

	Monday	Tuesday	Wednesday	Thursday	Friday	Saturday	Sunday
Breakfast							
Lunch							
Dinner							
Snacks							

Test Practice

Joe's Pit Stop

Sandwiches		*Sides*	
Hot Dog	$1.75	Potato Skins	$1.95
Hamburger	$2.25	French Fries	$1.95
Cheeseburger	$2.95	Onion Rings	$2.50
Cheese Steak	$4.95	Cole Slaw	$0.95
Grilled Chicken Sandwich	$4.95	Potato Chips	$0.50
Clam Strips	$5.95		
Lobster Roll	$7.75		

Condiments: mustard, relish, ketchup, mayo, lettuce, tomato, onion

Cheese --- $0.40 extra

1. Which of the following best describes the sandwiches at Joe's Pit Stop?

   (1) About 50% have seafood.

   (2) $\frac{1}{4}$ of the sandwiches have chicken.

   (3) $\frac{3}{4}$ of the sandwiches have cheese.

   (4) A hot dog costs about half of what a lobster roll does.

   (5) More than 75% of the sandwiches are served hot.

2. Which of the following best describes the side orders at Joe's Pit Stop?

   (1) $\frac{2}{3}$ of the sides cost less than a dollar.

   (2) About $\frac{1}{2}$ of the sides are made with vegetables.

   (3) $\frac{3}{5}$ of the sides are made with potatoes.

   (4) $\frac{3}{4}$ of the sides are served hot.

   (5) 25% of the sides are made with mayonnaise.

3. Joe has noticed that his business is not doing as well as it was last year. He wonders whether it is because people are becoming more health-conscious. Who should he ask to determine whether he should change his menu offerings?

   (1) He should ask his regular customers when they come in to buy something.

   (2) He should send a survey to people living in the area.

   (3) He should go to the mall and survey people who are shopping.

   (4) He should ask his family and friends what they like to eat.

   (5) He should send a survey to all the local area businesses.

4. Joe has begun to monitor what his customers are buying to make sure people want what he is selling. Over the past two weeks, he documented the following sales:

   Potato skins: 157

   French fries: 43

   Onion rings: 75

   Cole slaw: 198

   Potato chips: 45

   Which of the following conclusions could Joe make based on the data he collected?

   (1) People ordered potato skins more often than any of the other sides.

   (2) Cole slaw accounts for about half of the sides sold.

   (3) Customers prefer potato skins to onion rings, about 2 to 1.

   (4) Most people did not like hot sides.

   (5) The cheapest side was the most popular one.

5. Joe also kept track of what sandwiches his customers bought. Over the past two weeks, he documented the following sales:

   Hot dogs: 124

   Hamburgers: 423

   Cheeseburgers: 321

   Cheese steak sandwiches: 326

   Chicken sandwiches: 652

   Lobster rolls: 298

   Clam strips: 95

   Based on this information, what conclusions can Joe draw?

   (1) About 50% of the seafood sold was lobster.

   (2) About $\frac{1}{4}$ of the seafood sold was clams.

   (3) More than half of the burgers sold were cheeseburgers.

   (4) About 75% of all sandwiches sold were burgers.

   (5) Chicken sandwiches represented more than $\frac{1}{3}$ of all sandwiches sold.

6. Joe has been monitoring his weekly sales. One week his sales of sandwiches totaled $4,863. The sales of sides during the same week totaled $389. Joe uses 50% of his sales to pay for food supplies. What amount does this represent?

LESSON 3

Displaying Data in a New Way

How do bar graphs compare with circle graphs?

Frequency graphs are great tools for organizing data, but data are usually presented in **bar graphs** or **circle graphs**. In this lesson you will create bar graphs from frequency graphs. Bar graphs allow you to quickly see the totals in each category. You will learn why there is a *y*-axis for bar graphs. The ***y*-axis**, the line that runs up and down on the left or right side of a graph, saves you time counting. You will also create a very simple circle graph from your frequency graph.

Activity 1: Constructing a Bar Graph

1. Start with a frequency graph.
2. Draw a bar around each category. Color each bar with a different color.

   Uh-oh, you cannot see the number of x's.
3. Draw a vertical line on the left-hand side of your frequency graph. This is called a y-axis.
4. Look at how many x's are in your tallest bar.
5. Write the number. For example, if the tallest bar has 12 x's, then the point on the y-axis with the same height will also be 12.
6. Number the rest of the y-axis. Since you probably will not have a lot of space on the line, you might want to skip count—for example, 2, 4, 6, 8; or 5, 10, 15, 20. Try to keep the spaces equal.
7. Title the bar graph you just created.
8. At the bottom, write the color for each category.

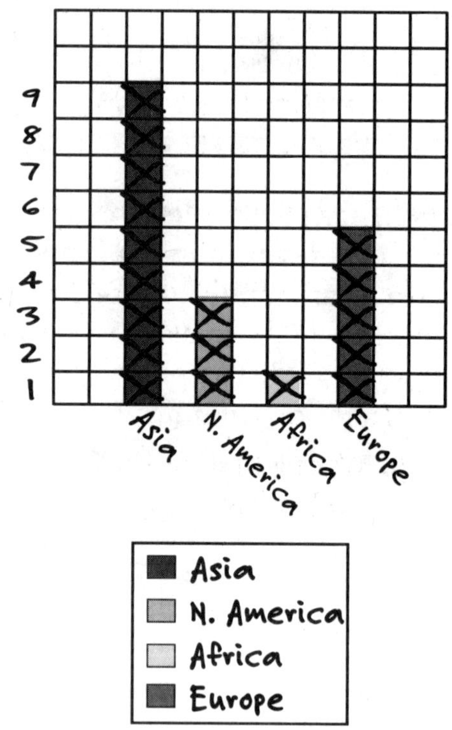

Activity 2: Constructing a Circle Graph

Follow these directions to create a circle graph from your bar graph.

1. Make a copy of the bar graph you just created.
2. Color each bar a different color.
3. Cut out the bars.
4. Tape the bars together, end-to-end, creating one long strip.
5. Create a circle from the strip by connecting the two ends.
6. Trace the circle onto a new piece of paper.

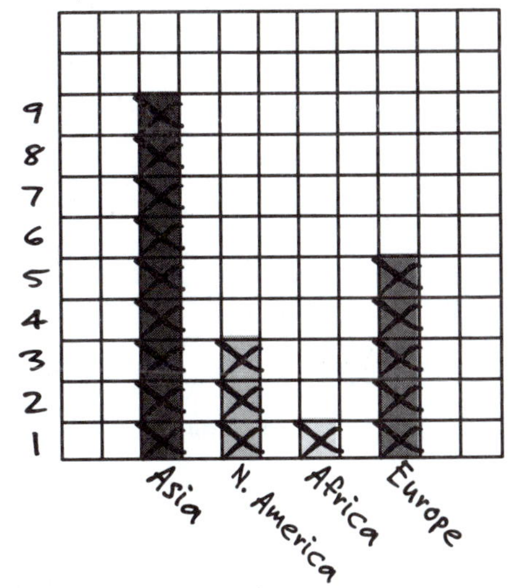

7. Mark off where each category begins and ends.

8. Draw a line from the center of the circle to the edge of the circle, creating pie slices for each different section.

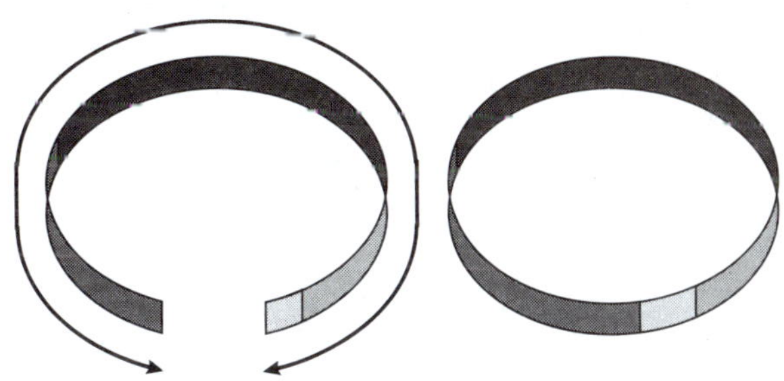

9. To keep track of the data, establish a legend or key, using one color for each bar. Record the legend next to the circle.

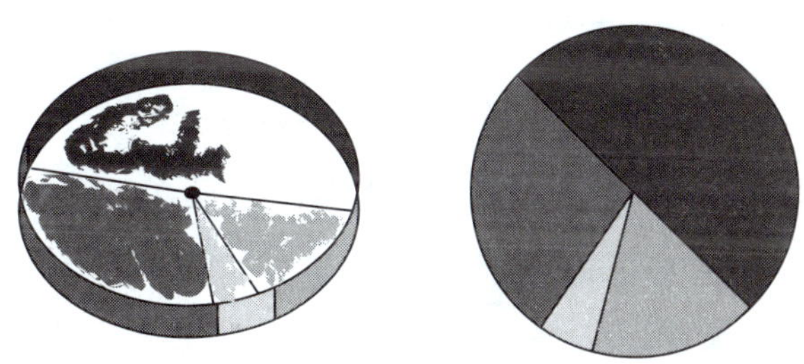

10. Write a title for your circle graph.

Practice: Label That *Y*-Axis

On each *y*-axis below, two or three numbers are given. Write the missing numbers in the boxes.

What should go on the **x-axis** (the horizontal line at the bottom)? You could have category names here or days of the week. You could also have numbers.

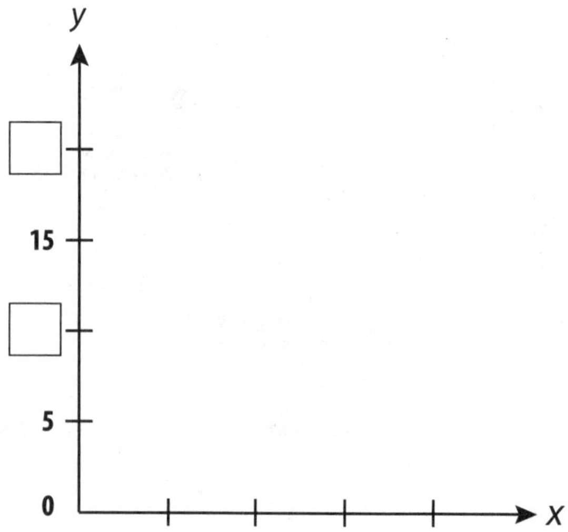

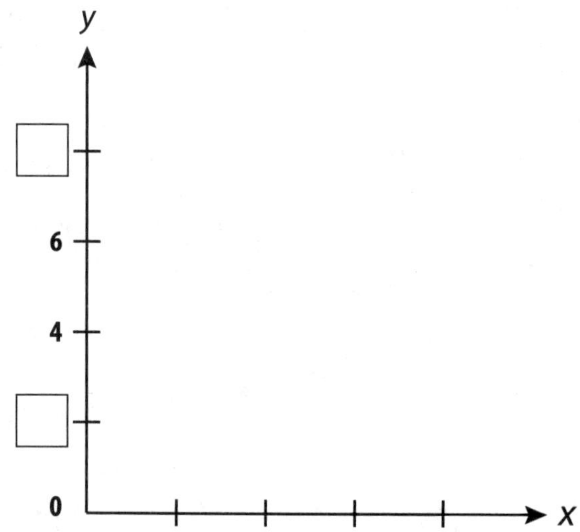

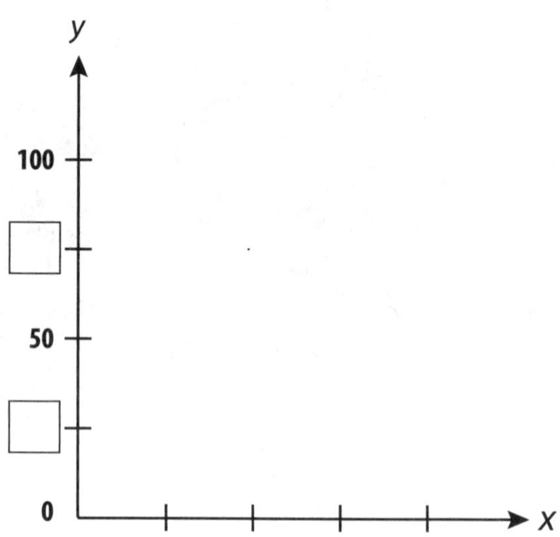

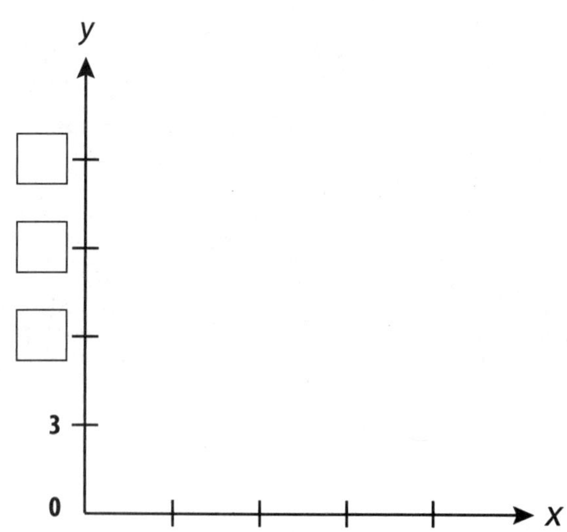

The two lines (*x*-axis and *y*-axis) usually meet at 0. Look at the number intervals you created. Do they increase or decrease in a way that makes sense? Practice reading the marks between numbers on a thermometer, stove dial, or another gauge.

Practice: Bar-Graph Details

1. Label the y-axis for the following bar graph:

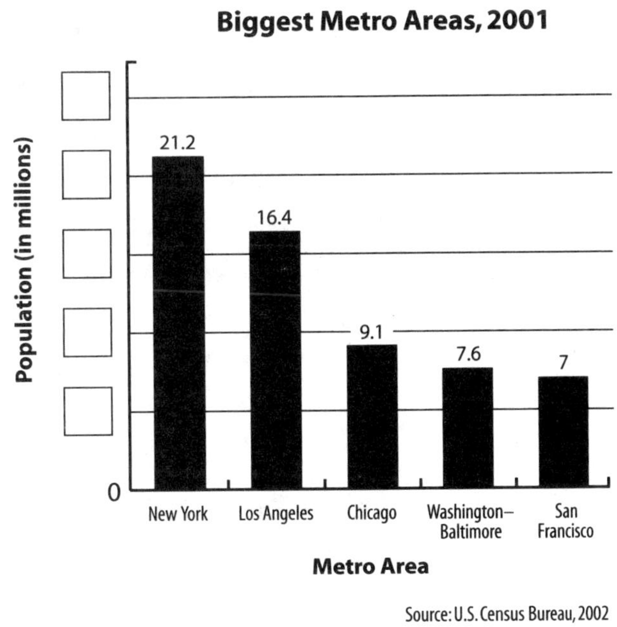

2. From the information on the graph, we can say that combined, the two biggest metro areas in California have a ______________ (smaller or larger) population than New York City. Chicago and Washington-Baltimore combined have about the same population as ______________________.

3. In these graphs, note that the y-axes have categories and the x-axes have numbers. Think of each one as a regular bar graph on its side.

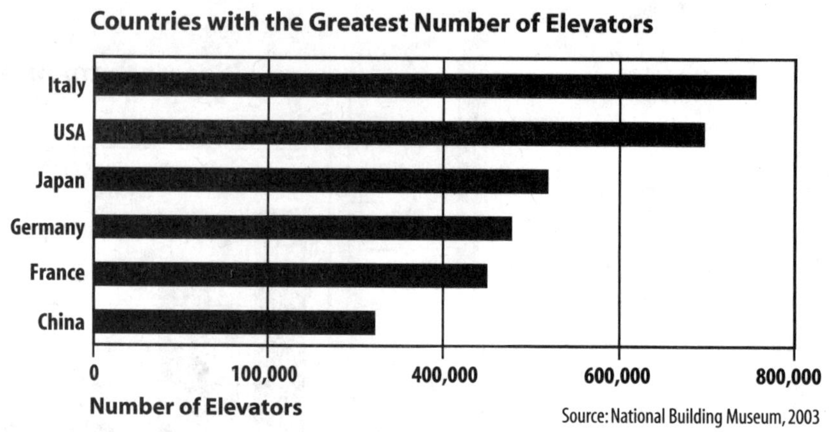

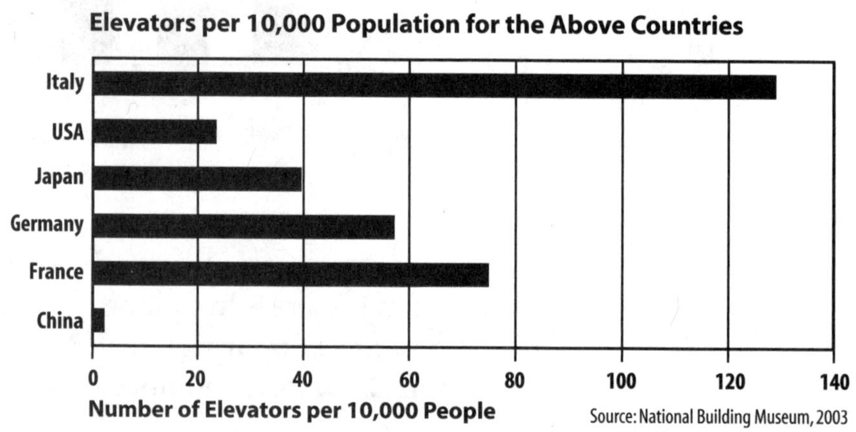

a. The first graph shows that ________________ has the greatest number of elevators; almost ________________ elevators.

b. ________________ has the second greatest number of elevators. However, in the second graph, it appears that this country does *not* have as many elevators per 10,000 people as do ________________, ________________, ________________, or ________________.

4. How would you explain China's small number of elevators in the second graph?

Practice: Bar Graph to Circle Graph

The following bar graph shows the causes of death for the 20,308 victims of homicide in the United States in 2001.

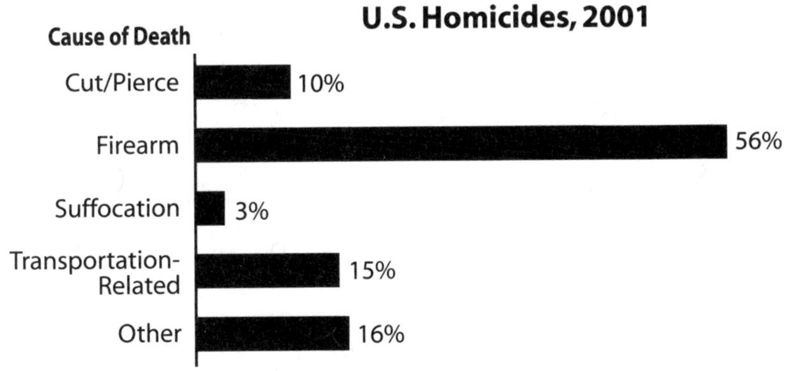

Source: Centers for Disease Control and Prevention, 2002

Using the data in the graph above, make a circle graph.

Give your circle graph a title, and label the slices.

Cut out the bars and tape them together to create a circle.

Extension: Foods You Eat in a Week

Research question: What foods do I eat in a week?

If you have been keeping track of what you eat, you are ready to do the project called "Foods You Eat in a Week."

The first step is to organize your data. If you are stuck for ideas, go back to *Lesson 2*. How did you and your class organize foods at that time? Brainstorm ideas with a classmate. Look at how foods are organized at the store.

Write a report on the types of foods you eat in a week. Your report should include

- The research question
- Two ways you categorized the data and an explanation of why you chose the ones you did
- A table with the data
- A frequency graph
- A bar graph
- A description of the results

When you describe the results, be sure to include

- At least two *true* statements about your data. Use percents or fractions in at least one of your statements.
- A statement or two summarizing your data. What do the data say about your eating habits?

Extension: Net Gains and Losses

In Massachusetts, it seems as though every day more houses and stores are built. Some sources say that Massachusetts lost an average of 29 acres of open land per day between 1985 and 1999. The graph below shows the changes in land use during that period.

Change in Land Use, 1985–1999 *(in acres)*

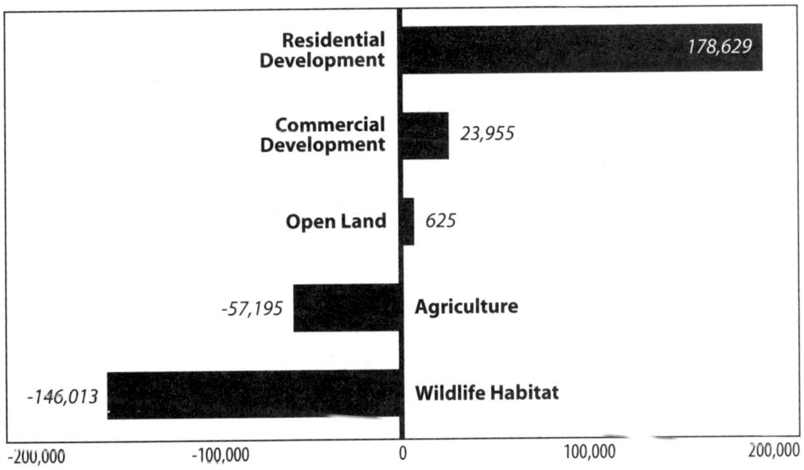

Source: Massachusetts Audubon Society, 2003

1. What do the labels on the x-axis represent?

2. What wildlife habitat net gains and/or losses do you see?

The bar graphs we have been looking at have had only positive values. This bar graph shows both positive (gains) and negative (losses) values. Note that the negative numbers increase as they move toward the left.

3. What is the largest net loss? How do you know?

4. What is the largest net gain? How do you know?

5. How do these net gains and losses compare to changes in land use in your state?

Test Practice

Items 1 and 2 are based on the graph below.

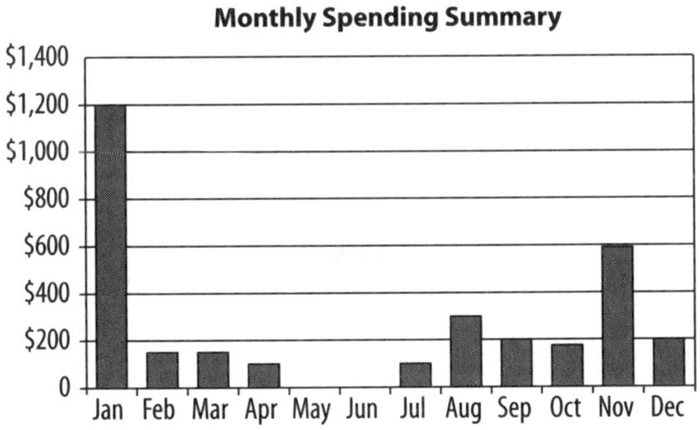

1. Based on Miguel's monthly spending summary above, what conclusions can you draw about how he used his credit card?
   (1) He probably went on shopping sprees once every three months.
   (2) He probably spent a lot of money just before the Christmas holidays.
   (3) He probably took a long time to pay off his account.
   (4) He probably had a very short vacation.
   (5) He probably bought a lot of back-to-school supplies in early fall.

2. According to the graph, which of the following statements is true?
   (1) There were more monthly expenditures the first half of the year than the second half.
   (2) There were more monthly expenditures the second half of the year than the first half.
   (3) In January, there were more expenditures than all other months combined.
   (4) There were no expenditures during the summer months.
   (5) About half of all the expenditures occurred during January.

Items 3 and 4 are based on the graph below.

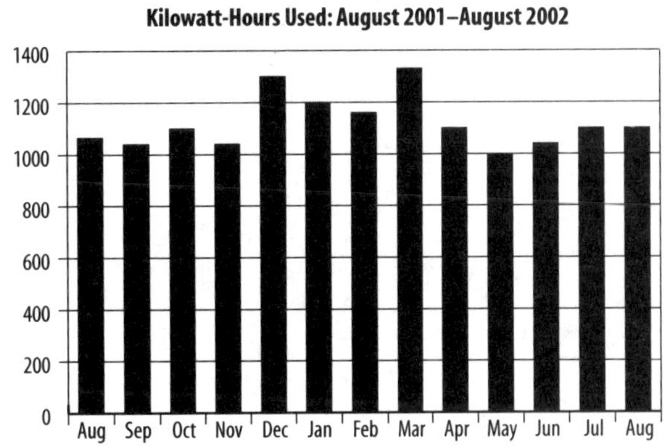

3. What conclusion can you draw from the information in the graph above?
   (1) More kilowatt-hours were used during the summer months than the winter months.
   (2) More kilowatt-hours were used during the winter months than the summer months.
   (3) More kilowatt-hours were used in August 2001 than in August 2002.
   (4) January 2002 was colder than February 2002.
   (5) August 2002 was warmer than August 2001.

4. Which of the statements below is *not* true based on the information in the graph?
   (1) More kilowatt-hours were used the last month in 2001 than the first month in 2002.
   (2) The fewest kilowatt-hours were used during the month of May.
   (3) At least 1,000 kilowatt-hours are used per month.
   (4) There were twice as many kilowatt-hours used in December as in May.
   (5) More than 12,000 kilowatt-hours were used over a 12-month period.

Items 5 and 6 are based on the following graph.

Cause of Death by Suicide in the United States, 2001

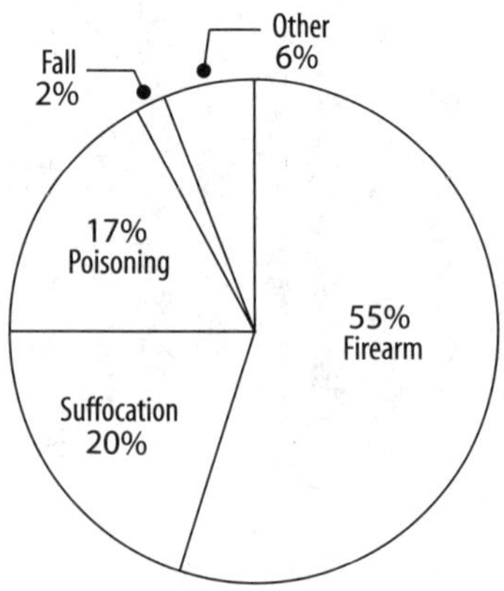

5. Which of the following statements about suicides in the United States in 2001 is true?

   (1) More than half of the suicides were by suffocation.

   (2) Less than a fourth of the suicides were by firearm.

   (3) Three-fourths of the suicides were either by firearm or suffocation.

   (4) About a quarter of the suicides were by poisoning.

   (5) There were more suicides by fall than by poisoning.

6. There were 30,622 suicides in the United States in 2001. Of those, 55% were by firearm. What percent were the other causes of death by suicide?

LESSON 4

A Closer Look at Circle Graphs

How can you tell what percent of the data are in each slice?

In this lesson, you will take a closer look at circle graphs. Circle graphs are sometimes called "pie charts" because they show what part of the total "pie" each category, or "slice," represents.

This lesson focuses on estimating the sizes of slices in order to sketch and interpret circle graphs.

It is important to be able to see quickly how items in a circle graph relate to each other. Is there one slice that represents about a half, or 50%? One that is about 25%? In this lesson you will estimate sizes of slices using benchmark percents.

Activity 1: How Many of Each?

1. How many women and men are there in your class?

	How Many	Fraction of Total	Benchmark Percent
Men			
Women			
Total			

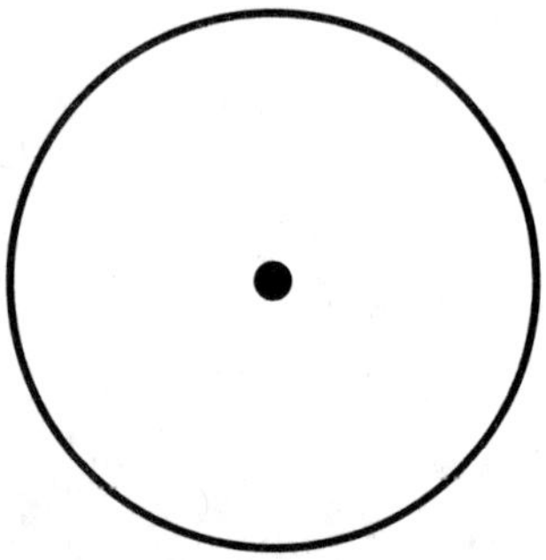

Sketch a circle graph to show how the number of men and the number of women relate to the total number of people in the class. Be sure to label each slice.

Check your work by asking yourself these questions:

- Are there more women or men? Is the larger slice the one that has the greatest number of people in it?
- Are there an equal number of men and women? If so, does your circle graph show two equal slices?
- Are there only men or only women in your class? If so, does your graph show that?
- If you made a bar graph, how do the bar heights compare?

What percent is the whole circle?

How do you know?

2. Conduct a quick poll that has only two possible answers. Questions you might ask include

- Werc you born in the United States?
- Did you see any movies in the last month?

	How Many	Fraction of Total	Benchmark Percent
Total			

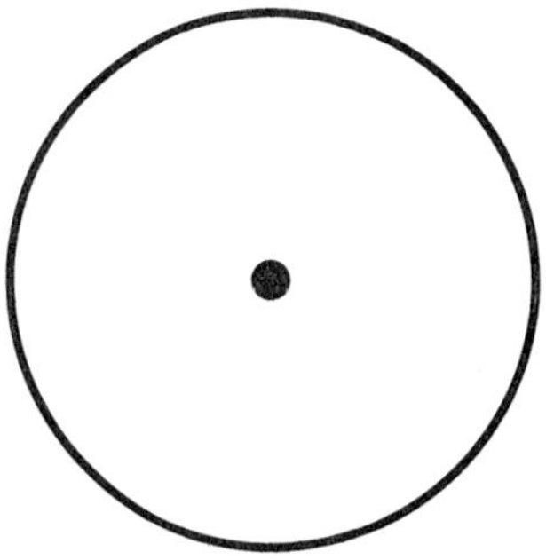

My question is

Sketch a circle graph to show the relationship of the number in each category to the total number. Be sure to label each slice.

What is the total number?

What is the total percent?

Activity 2: Cheat Sheet

Fill in the appropriate percent for each slice.

(1)
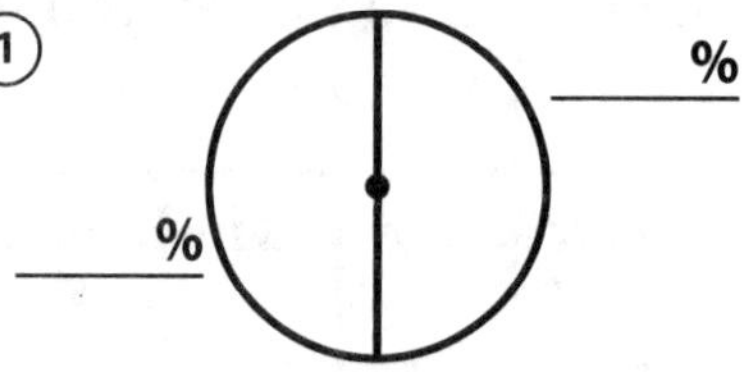

(2)
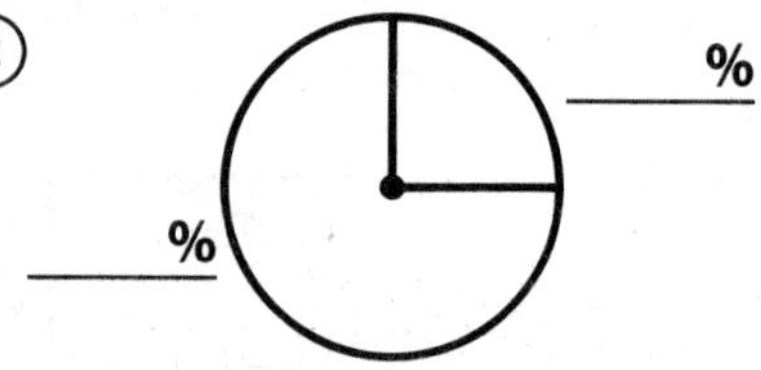

(3)
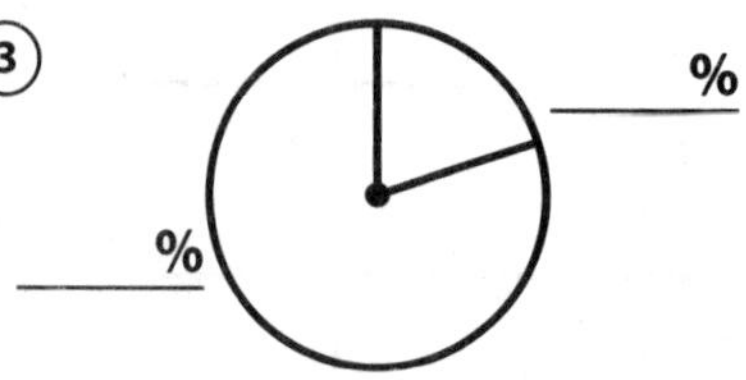

(4)
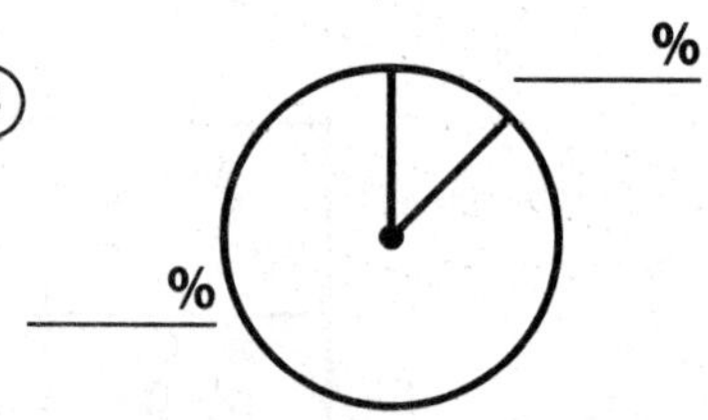

(5)
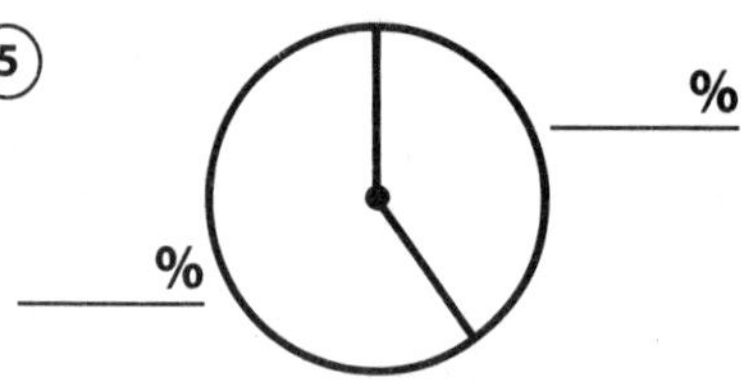

(6)
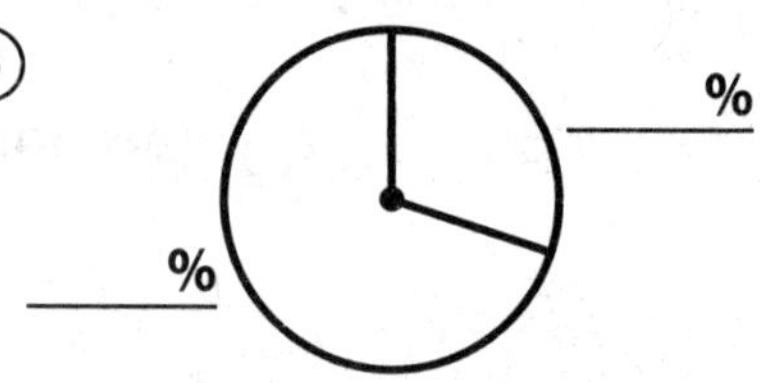

(7)
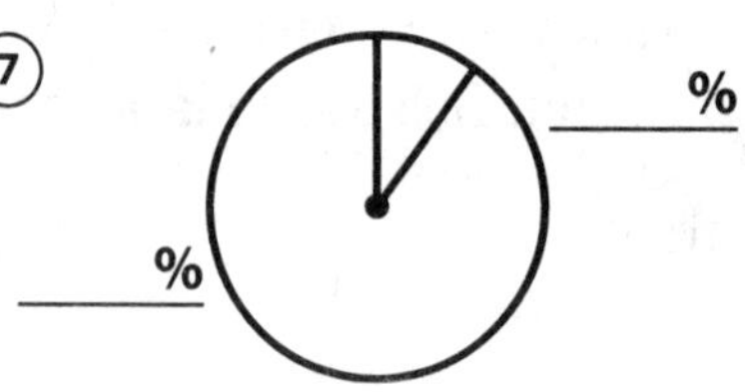

If you need a hint, see page 53.

Choose three of the circles above and show their percents, using different starting points on the circles below to create new slices. For example, for 50%:

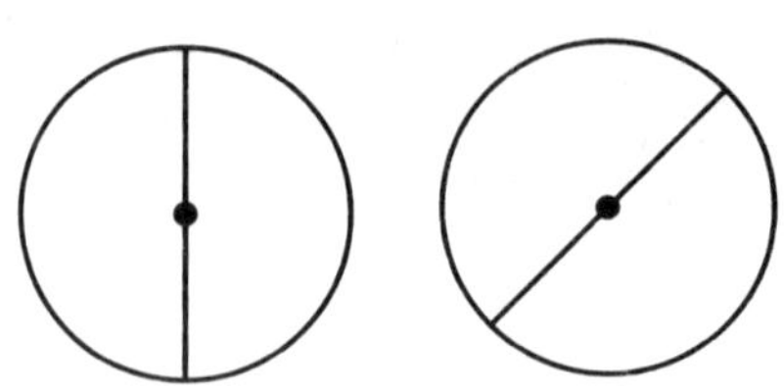

Activity 3: Three Possible Answers

1. The first question we asked: ______________________________

Category	How Many	Fraction of Total	Benchmark Percent
Total			

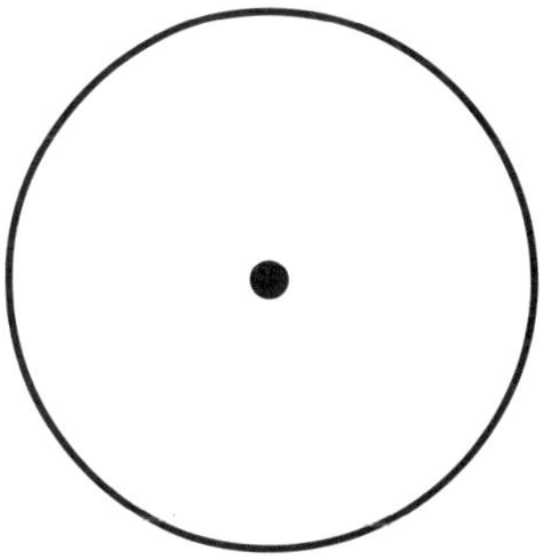

Now convert the data you collected to a circle graph.

Write the graph title and label the slices.

2. The second question we asked: ______________________________

Category	How Many	Fraction of Total	Benchmark Percent
Total			

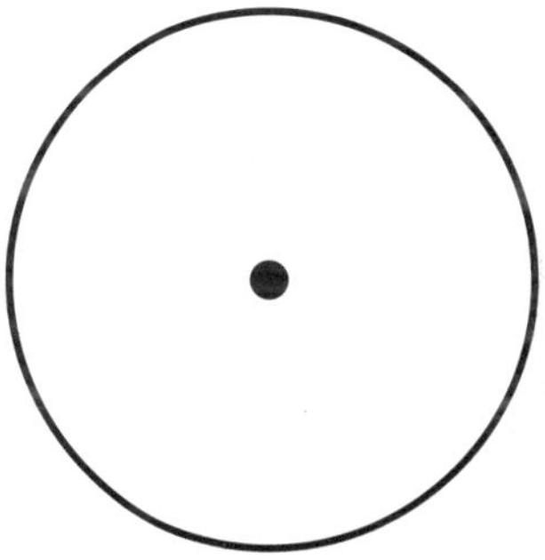

Now convert the data you collected to a circle graph.

Write the graph title and label the slices.

3. The circle graphs below represent responses to a questionnaire mailed to citizens of four different towns.

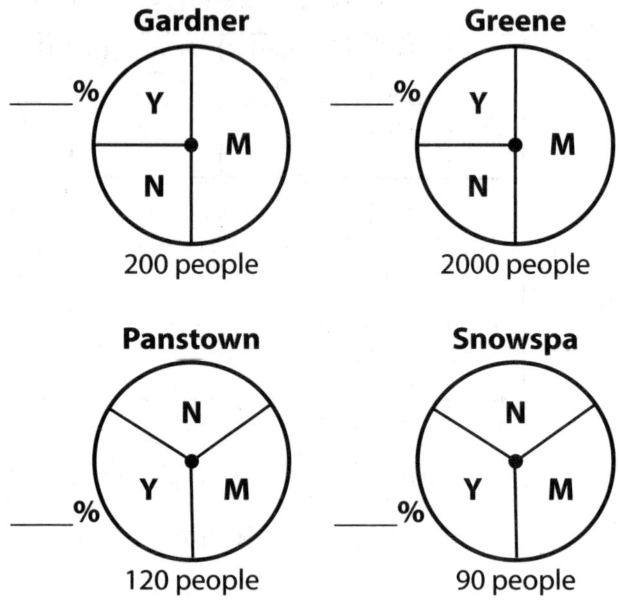

a. Write the percent that voted Y(yes) for each town.

b. What town had the most yes votes?

c. What town had the least yes votes?

d. How do you know?

e. Is this what you expected? Why?

When figuring out how to interpret a circle graph, try this:

Draw a line to slice the chart in half.

Ask yourself: Is the biggest slice more than, less than, or equal to half?

Draw another line that cuts the circle into four equal parts. Ask yourself: Is any slice close to 25%?

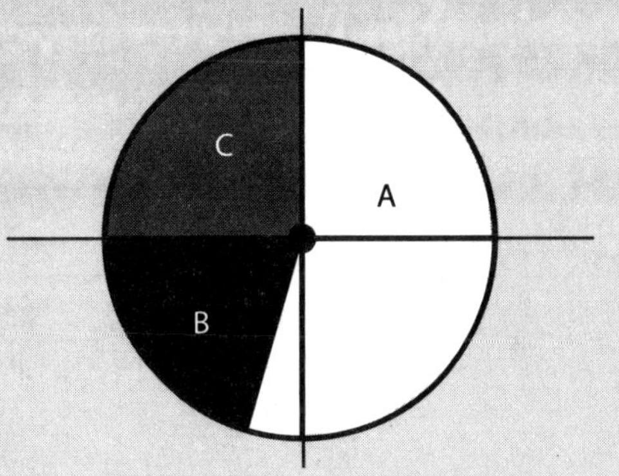

Practice: Estimating Percents and Parts of the Whole

Estimate the percent of each of the categories in the circle graphs below.

1. A is about __________ %.

B is about __________ %.

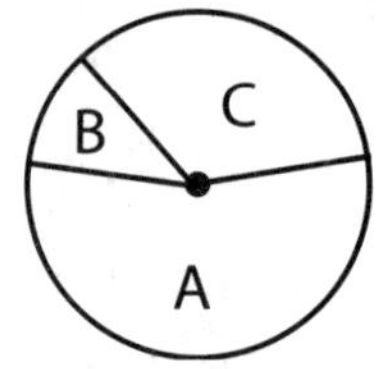

2. A is about __________ %.

C is about __________ %.

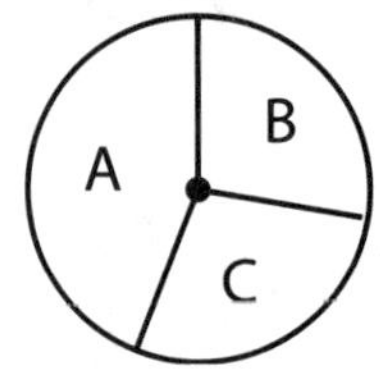

3. A is about __________ %.

B is about __________ %.

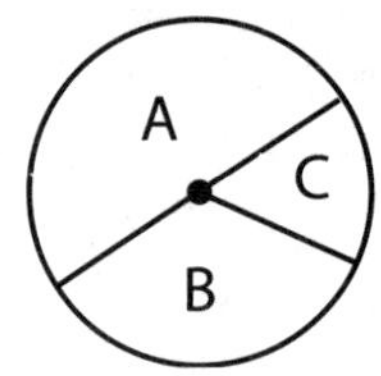

4. A is about __________ %.

B is about __________ %.

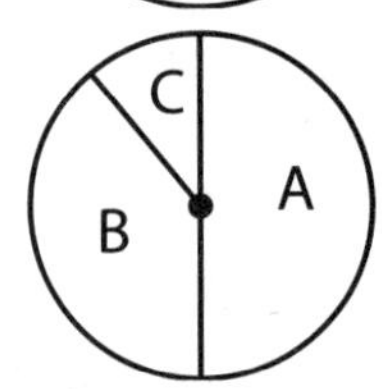

Shade the appropriate parts of the circles for these percents or fractions.

5. A = 40%

B = 60%

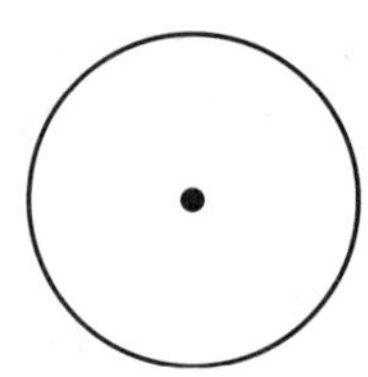

6. $A = \frac{2}{3}$

$B = \frac{1}{3}$

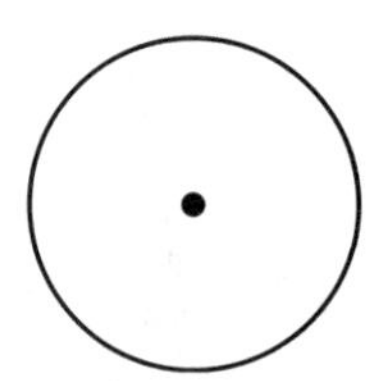

7. A = 25%

B = 10%

C = 65%

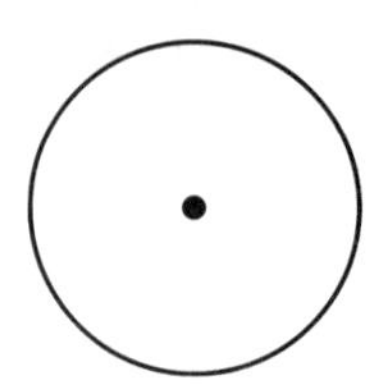

8. $A = \frac{1}{4}$

$B = \frac{1}{2}$

C = _____ (You complete it!)

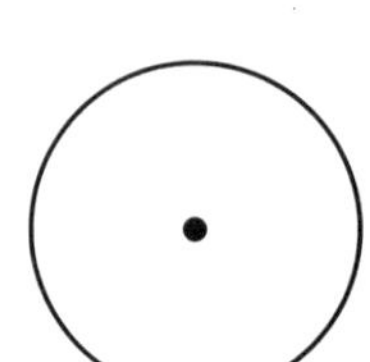

Practice: Serve Up the Pie

You work for a local paper that publishes fun statistics every week. Your job is to serve up the pie graphs. Design a circle graph to go with each of the following data sets.

1. A group of people was asked about their favorite ice cream flavors. The results are shown here:

Using the information from the bar graph, complete this table:

Flavor	How Many	Fraction of Total	Benchmark Percent
Chocolate			
Vanilla			
Strawberry			
Total			

Sketch a circle graph of the categories.

Label or color-code each slice.

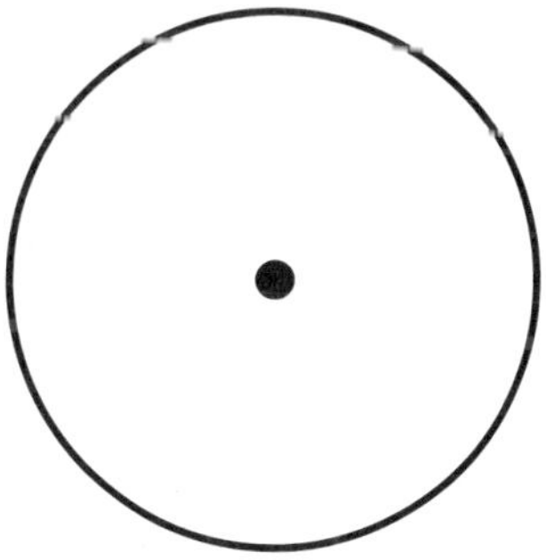

Practice: Serve Up the Pie *(continued)*

2. In a portable heater factory, workers check the heaters for quality control. During the week of June 7, 2002, the total number of heater defects were as shown in this bar graph:

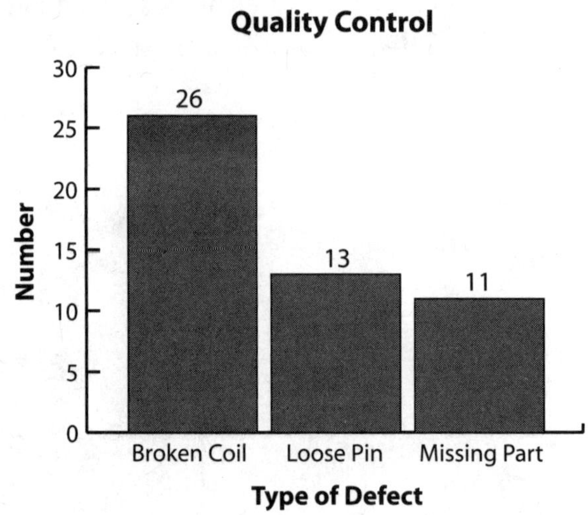

Using the information from the bar graph, complete the table:

Type of Defect	How Many	Fraction of Total	Benchmark Percent
Broken Coil			
Loose Pin			
Missing Part			
Total			

Sketch a circle graph of the defect types.

Label or color-code each slice.

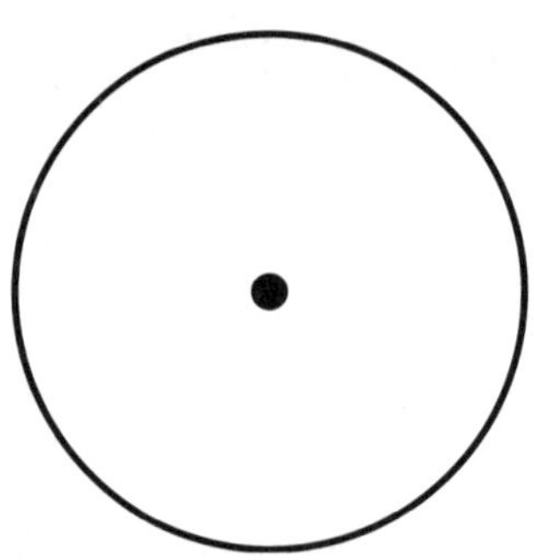

3. The registered voters in Green Gulch are shown in this graph:

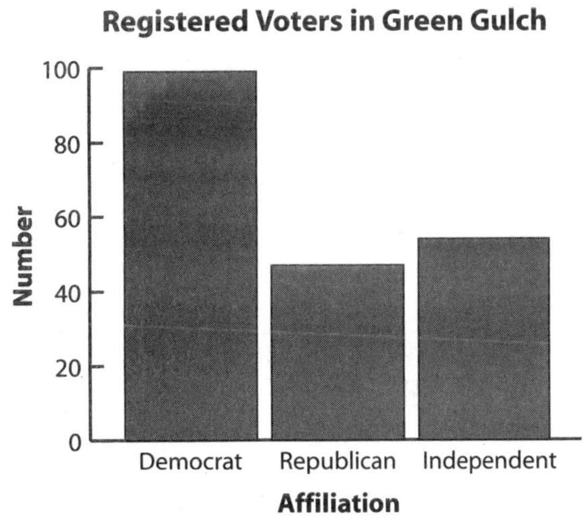

Using the information from the bar graph, complete the table:

Affiliation	How Many	Fraction of Total	Benchmark Percent
Republican			
Democrat			
Independent			
Total			

Sketch a circle graph of the affiliations.

Label or color-code each slice.

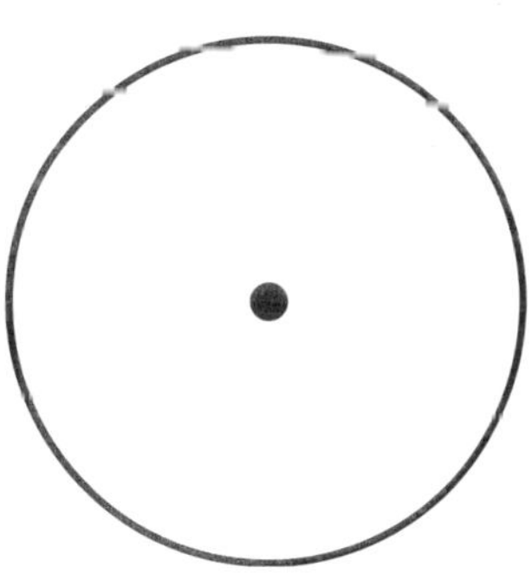

Practice: Making Predictions

Think about how the graph below could be interpreted in order to make predictions about the data. Then answer the questions.

Sri is the manager of a shoe store. She conducted a recent survey to determine which color sandal people liked best for summer, then created a circle graph of the results.

Sandal Colors

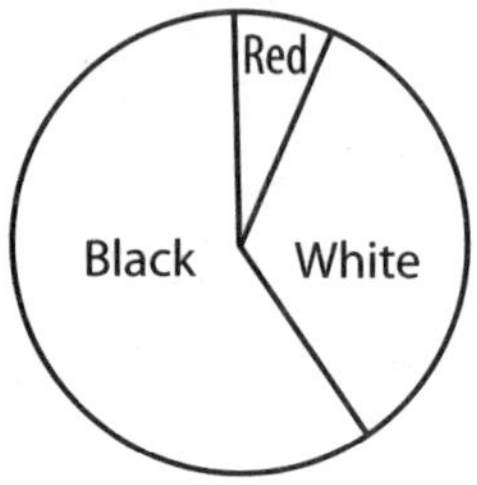

1. Which color would you recommend she order the most of?

    ____

2. Which color might she consider not buying? ________________

The graph below shows the percent of different colors in each bag of Beady Balls Candy.

Beady Ball Candy Colors

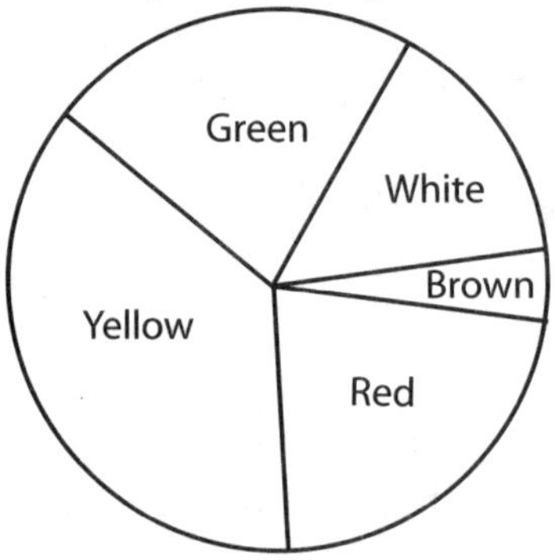

3. If you were to pick one candy out of the bag without looking, which color would you most likely pick? ________________

4. If you picked a candy out of the bag without looking, which color would you be least likely to pick? ________________

Extension: The Computer Makes the Graph

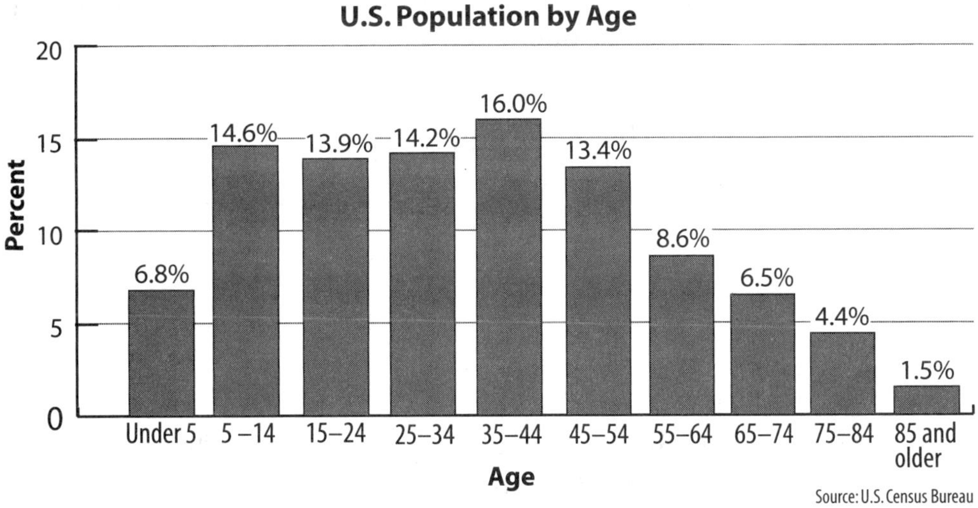

Collapse the "U.S. Population by Age" data into three categories, and list the categories.

People in many kinds of jobs make presentations with graphs and tables. If they have access to computers, they organize and enter the data, and the computer does the work of constructing a graph.

If you have Microsoft® Excel on a computer, use it to make a circle graph for these data (for help with Microsoft Excel, see *Spreadsheet Guide*, pages 154–155).

If you do not have a computer, sketch the circle graph based on your three categories.

Write three statements about the "U.S. Population by Age" data using benchmark fractions or percents, based on the circle graph you made.

Extension: Search for Circle Graphs

Look through publications at home, at work, in waiting rooms you visit, or in the magazine section of the library. Find examples of circle graphs and choose one. Then answer the questions below based on the circle graph you chose.

1. What is the graph about?

2. Is the total number of items reported somewhere in the graph or not? How do you know?

3. Is the data from a random sample or not? How do you know?

4. Were you able to estimate the size of each slice before finding out the actual percent?

Test Practice

1. According to the chart below, which of the following represented over half of the TV parts sold in January?
   (1) Flat tube 32″ and flat tube 52″
   (2) Flat tube 32″ and pocket LCD
   (3) Flat tube 52″ and widescreen 32″
   (4) Widescreen 32″ and flat tube 32″
   (5) Pocket LCD

2. According to the chart below, which of the following represents just over one-quarter of the TV parts sold in January?
   (1) Widescreen 32″
   (2) Pocket LCD
   (3) Flat tube 52″
   (4) Flat tube 32″
   (5) Flat tube 32″ and Flat tube 52″

3. According to the graph below, which blood type would a blood donor be least likely to have?
   (1) A-
   (2) B+
   (3) B-
   (4) AB+
   (5) AB-

4. According to the graph below, which of the following blood types represents just over three-quarters of the donors?
   (1) O- and O+ and B+
   (2) O+ and A+ and A-
   (3) O- and A- and B-
   (4) O+ and O- and A-
   (5) A+ and AB-

Product Models Sold in January

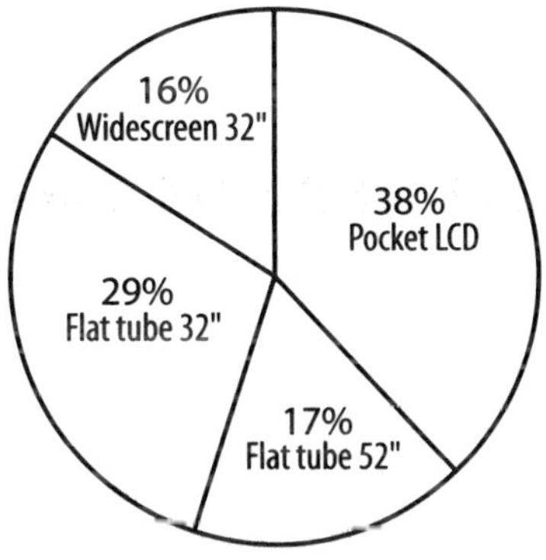

Donors' Blood Types

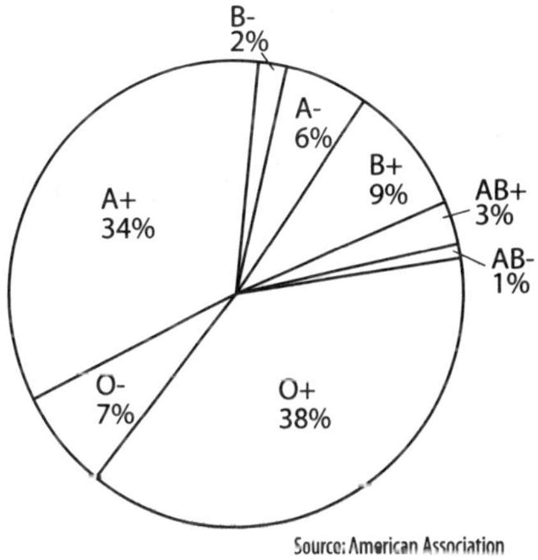

Source: American Association of Blood Banks, 2003

5. According to the graph below, which of the following candidates received just over half of all the votes in Westside's town election?

(1) Rivera

(2) Blake and Rivera

(3) Blake and Ling

(4) Ling and Smith

(5) Rivera and Smith

Westside Town Election 2002

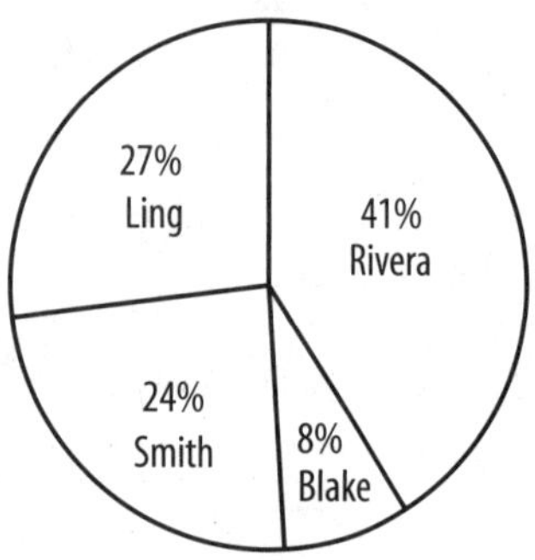

6. Use a calculator to answer the following question: If the number of voters in Westside was 40,000, how many votes did Smith capture?

LESSON 5

Sketch This

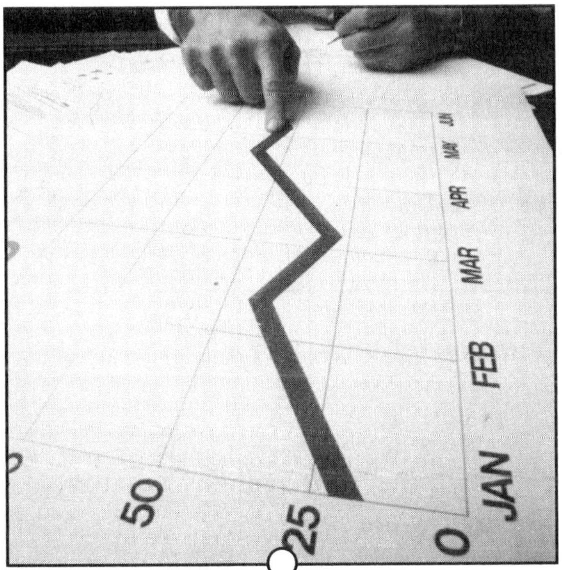

Words can tell a story, but so can lines.

In this lesson, you will learn about **line graphs**. Line graphs often show change over time. Sometimes line graphs are called trend graphs because they show a trend or tell a story about the direction and rate of change (or the absence of change).

You will look closely at the shape of a line graph to get clues about what has been happening over time: Has there been a change? If so, was it an increase or a decrease? You will also use labels to give you further clues.

Using the shape of the line and the labels and numbers on the x- and y-axes, you can quickly get a general interpretation of a line graph.

Activity 1: Sketch This

Read the statement below. Sketch a line in the "L" that shows what is happening in the story. Let your line follow the story.

- The river swelled during five days of rain. Monday, Tuesday, and Wednesday there was a steady rain. Thursday it poured, and Friday the rain came down as a soft drizzle. The water level rose over these five days.

Find a partner and discuss why you each sketched the graph the way you did. As you talk about the graphs, think about the words you use to describe them. Jot down those descriptive words.

Activity 2: Label This

Work with your classmates to label the axes and title the graphs you have made so far.

Practice: Candy Bars

Each of the graphs below could represent the cost of candy bars over the past 10 years. Match the statement with the graph that best represents it. Write the letter of the matching statement on the line below the graph.

1. The price of a candy bar has risen dramatically over the past 10 years.
2. The price of a candy bar has decreased over the past 10 years.
3. The price of a candy bar has fluctuated (increased and decreased) over the past 10 years.
4. The price of a candy bar has slowly, but steadily, increased over the past 10 years.

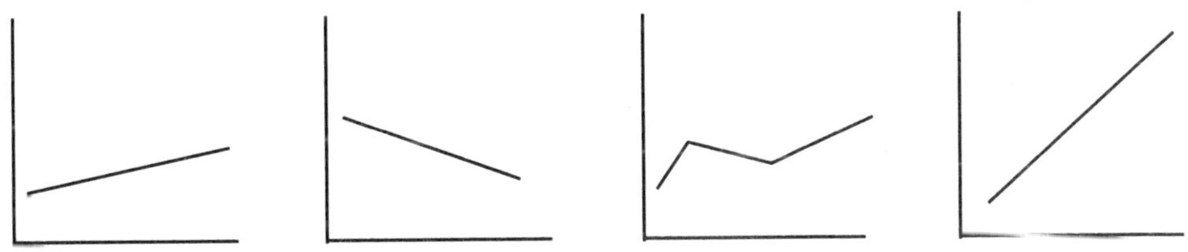

_______ _______ _______ _______

Compare the graphs to the statements. What words gave you a clue about the shape of the graph?

Can you think of another statement that could describe the cost of a candy bar over the past 10 years? How would a graph of that statement look in comparison to the graphs above?

Practice: How Does It Go?

Sketch a line that illustrates the following:

> "The weather was crazy today! It was very cold in the morning, then it warmed up, and by lunchtime it was hot. In the early afternoon, a dark cloud covered the sky, and by 4 p.m. it was raining and chilly. It rained hard, but by dinnertime it had stopped. The evening was pleasant."

When you are trying to figure out how to interpret the shape of a line graph, be sure to look at the *x*- and *y*-axes for clues. Just because a line goes up (**increases**) does not mean that the change is a good one. A line going down (**decreases**) does not always mean that something is a loss (or negative). Look at these two examples:

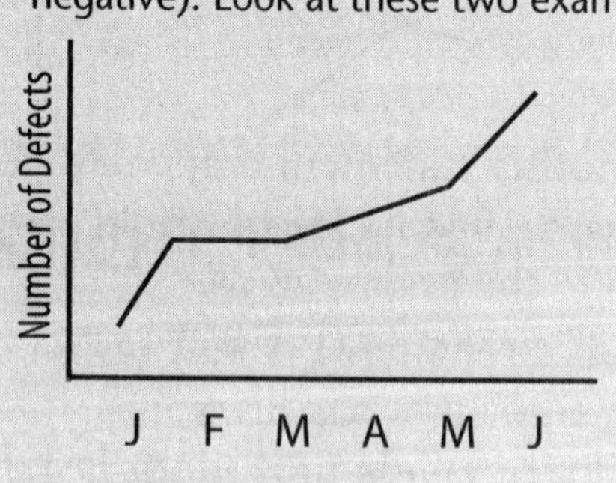

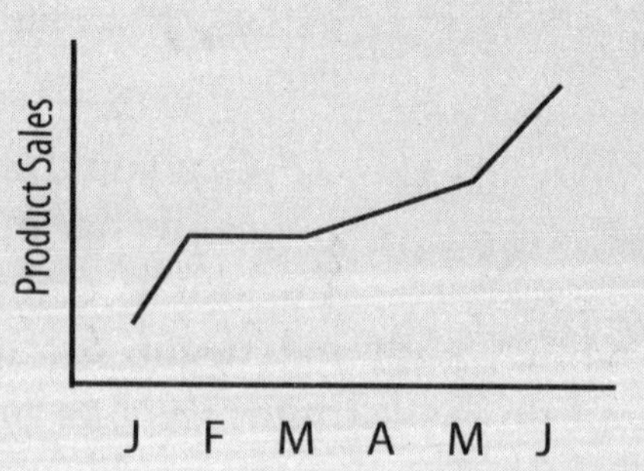

If you get stuck trying to read the labels along the *x*-axis, remember that the graph is about time. Think about which labels are used with time. They could be related to days, weeks, months, or quarters of years.

When you sketch a line graph, think about the line at three stages in time. First, think about how it begins. Then think about what happens next. How does the line change, if at all? Finally, think about how it ends in relation to where it began.

Practice: Looking at the Entire Graph

Decide which graph in each set best answers the question. Write the letter for the graph on the blank line at the end of the question.

1. Which of the following graphs shows a decrease in the number of defects the first week and then no change the second week?

 ____

A.
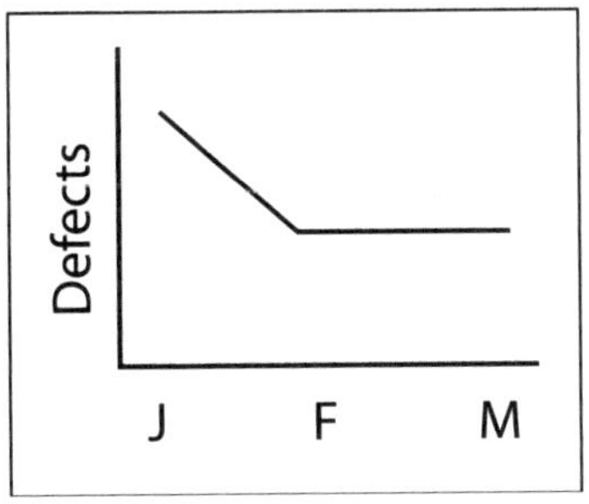

B.

C.
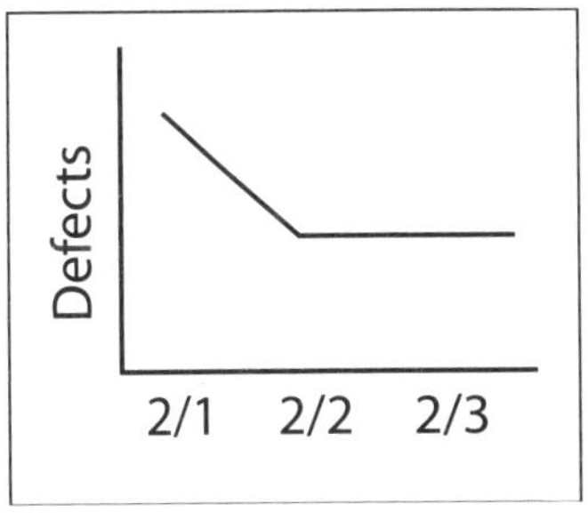

2. Which of the following graphs, over time, could a restaurant manager use to decide which day each week her café should be closed for cleaning? ___________

A.
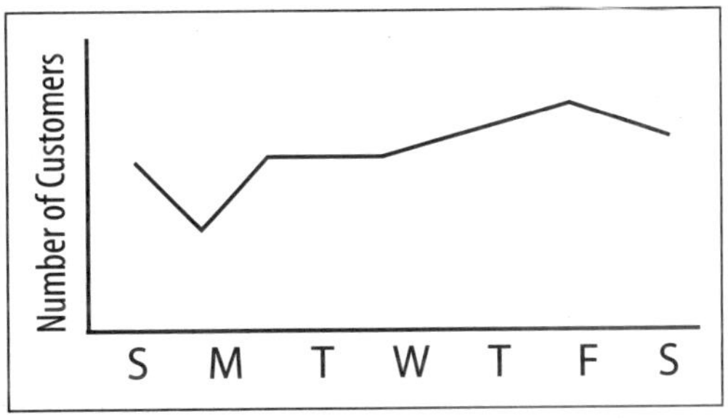

B.
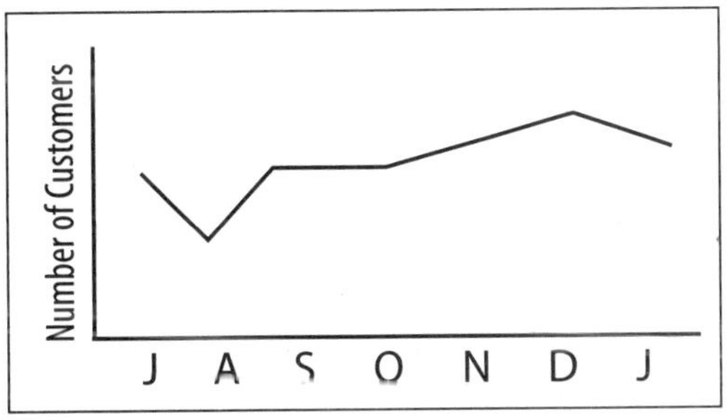

C.
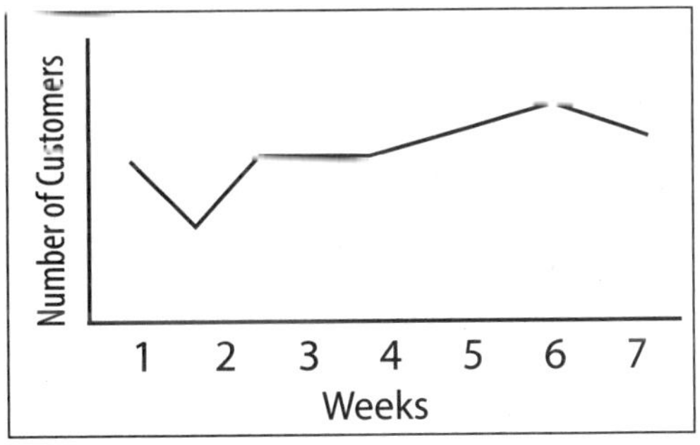

Practice: Labeling Graphs

For each graph below, decide on an appropriate set of labels based on the information provided. Write your labels on the lines along the x-axis.

1. Sales dropped slightly from March to April, then increased dramatically the next month.

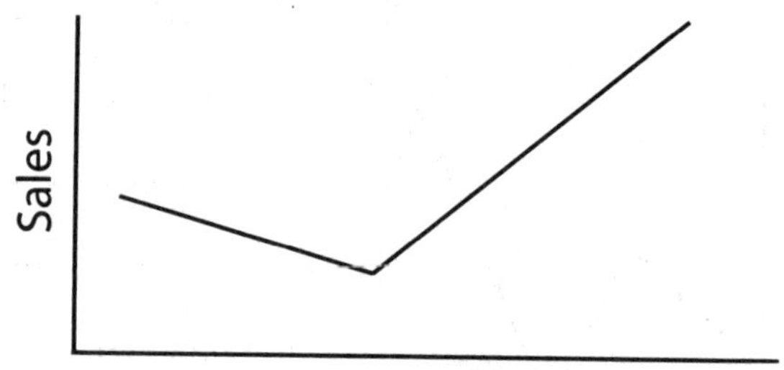

2. For the week of March 19, Franklin Factory steadily increased the number of products assembled daily, except on Friday, when production dropped.

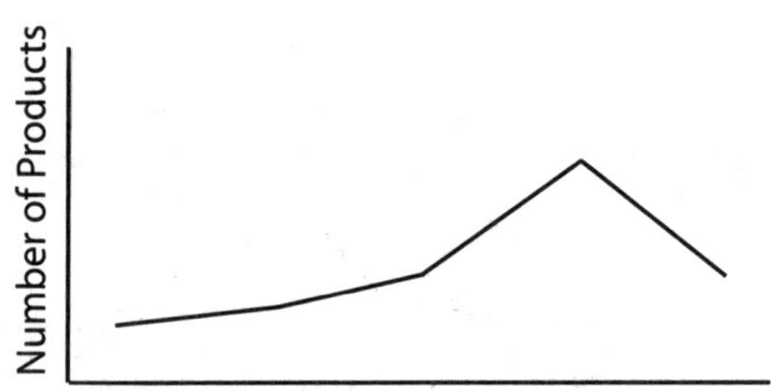

Practice: Telling a Story

For each of the graphs below, create a story that fits the shape of the graph. You may want to include information on the x-axis to support your story.

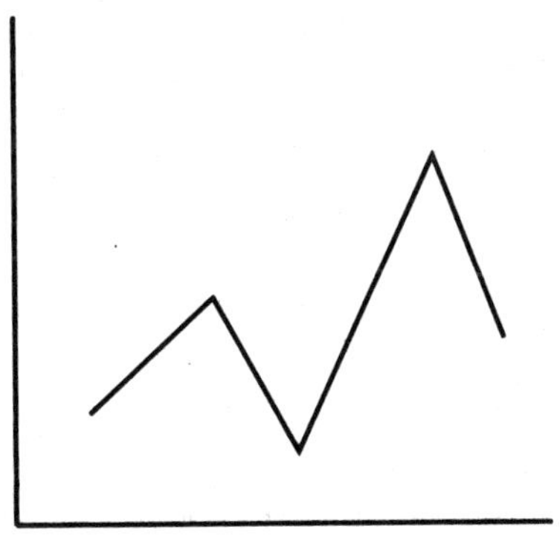

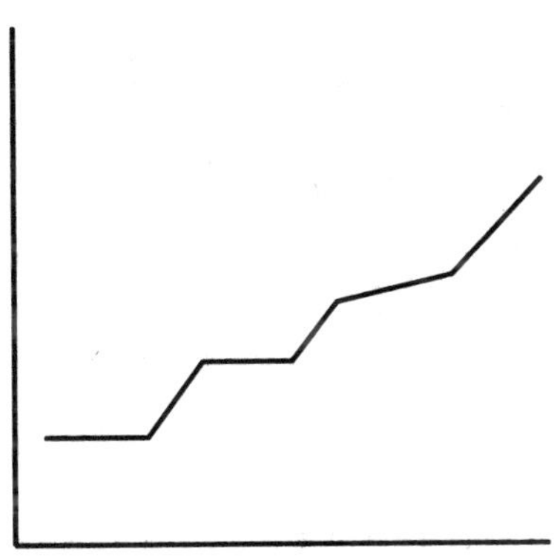

Extension: The Shape of a Line from Your Life

Think of an event from your own life that has occurred over time. Sketch what it should look like. Remember that the shape of the graph should give you an idea about what happened over time.

Extension: Elevator Traffic

The following graph shows the elevator traffic in the Chicago Prudential Building in 2000, when 27 elevators completed an estimated 60,000 passenger rides every day.

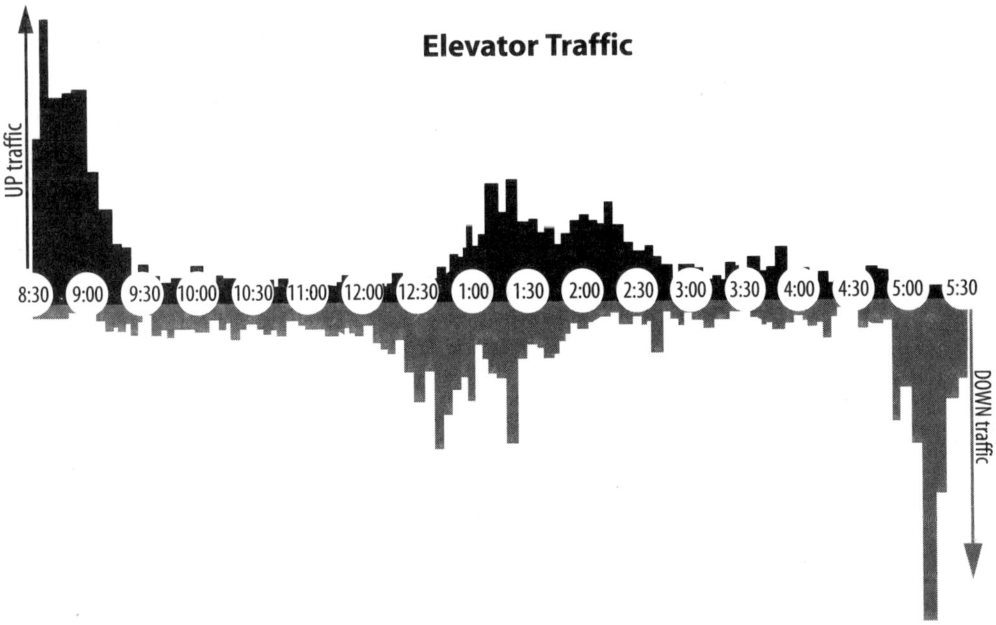

Source: The National Building Museum, 2003

What do you notice about the elevator traffic? Tell the story of the graph.

Test Practice

Items 1 and 2 refer to "My House Every Day."

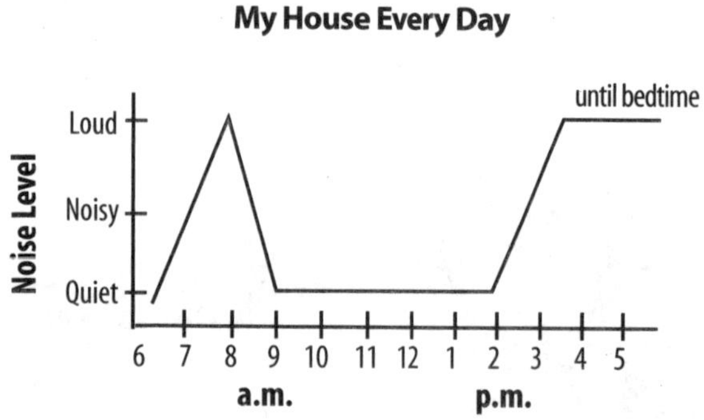

Adapted from field test student work

1. According to the graph, noise increases steadily in the morning from
   (1) 6:00 to 8:00
   (2) 6:00 to 9:00
   (3) 6:30 to 9:00
   (4) 8:30 to 9:00
   (5) 8:00 to 9:00

2. Which statement is *not* true of the period of greatest quiet: The period of greatest quiet is
   (1) The longest time frame on the graph.
   (2) Only occurs during the afternoon hours.
   (3) Is followed by a steady increase in noise.
   (4) Is not totally silent.
   (5) Is about five hours long.

Items 3 and 4 refer to "Weight."

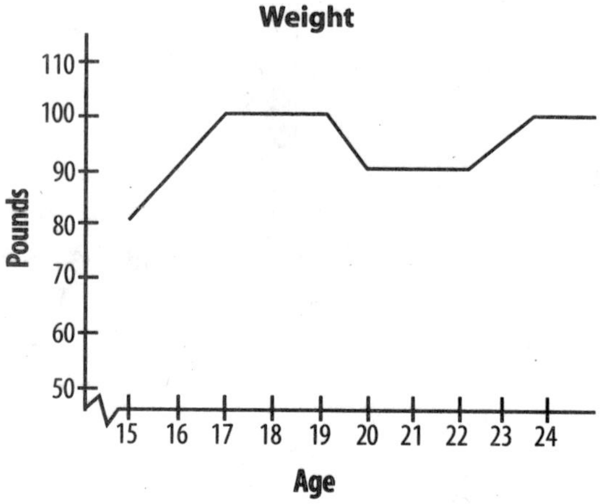

Adapted from field test student work

3. At what age(s) was the woman at her lowest weight?
   (1) 15
   (2) 17
   (3) 18
   (4) 20
   (5) 21

4. According to the graph, the woman gained over 20 pounds between which birthdays?
   (1) 15th and 16th
   (2) 16th and 17th
   (3) 15th and 17th
   (4) 17th and 18th
   (5) 17th and 19th

Items 5 and 6 refer to "Immigration from China 1850–1900."

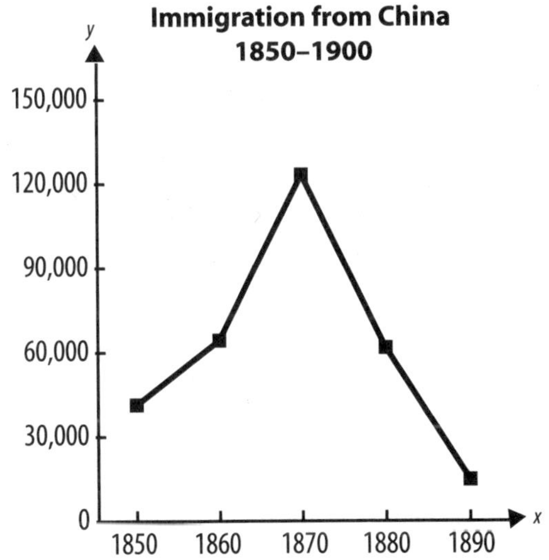

Source: U.S. Department of Homeland Security, 2003

5. The graph shows that the pattern of immigration from China

   (1) Peaked in 1860.

   (2) Doubled and then declined.

   (3) Tripled and then declined.

   (4) Had the least change in the 1860s and 1870s.

   (5) Between 1850 and 1900 was never less than 20,000 immigrants per year.

6. The graph represents data from how many decades?

LESSON 6

Roller-Coaster Rides

What story does the graph tell?

In this lesson, you will use precise vocabulary to make and analyze statements about line graphs that show **change over time**. You will learn phrases such as "steep increase" and "rapid decrease" to describe line graphs. When you understand how to use words effectively, you can influence others' decisions. You will also learn to question whether decisions or predictions can be made based on the information presented.

When describing a line graph, think of it at three points in time:

At the beginning ...

Then ...

Toward the end ...

Keep your language precise. Use words to make the general idea such as "goes up" or "goes down" more specific. For example, instead of saying that a salary increased between 1990 and 2000, state more precisely that it increased by $5,000 between 1990 and 2000; or the increase between 1999 and 2000 was twice as much as the increase between 1980 and 1990; or there was a dramatic increase between 1970 and 1975.

Activity 1: Amusement Park Attendance

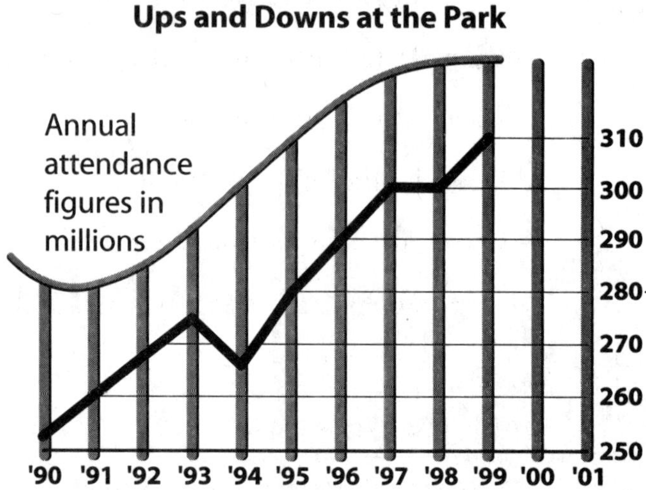

Source: *The Boston Sunday Herald*, June 4, 2000

1. Describe what you see in the graph.

2. Make two statements that are true descriptions or inferences based on the graph.

3. Make one statement that is a false description or inference based on the graph.

Activity 2: (Stations 1 and 2) Ups and Downs

You will work with a partner on this activity.

Student 1: Tell the story of the graph.

Start with "This graph is about..."

Describe the shape of the lines.

Use words like "doubled" or "increased by $0.50."

Give your partner time to sketch the graph based on your story.

Student 2: Draw the graph.

Listen to the story of the graph.

Sketch the graph, as you did in the last lesson.

Label and title your sketch.

Students 1 and 2: When the sketch is completed,

Look at the graph together.

Talk about how the sketch and the graph are the same and how they are different.

Review the description and talk about which statements were difficult to phrase or hard to understand or sketch, and which were clear.

Make notes on the most helpful words.

When you move to the next station, switch roles.

Notes:

Activity 2: (Station 3) Jerri's Jobs

Jerri has done freelance work for Jeff's Janitorial Service for five years. At the end of every year, she receives a 1099 form from them to submit with her taxes.

Use the nonemployee compensation shown on the 1099 forms to make a graph of Jerri's earnings from 1999 to 2003. Then answer the questions below. Make sure to show an amount for every year.

1. Between what two years did the greatest change occur?

2. When did Jerri's earnings decrease by almost half?

3. The most surprising thing about this graph is

4. Use numbers and words to describe the difference between her earnings for 1999 and 2003.

Activity 2: (Station 4) The Price of a Subway Ride

Use the information on the price of a subway token to create a graph.

- Make an x- and a y- axis.
- Label the axes.
- Have someone check your work before you continue.
- Put a point on the graph for each time the price of a token changed.
- Talk with a partner about why simply connecting the points with a line will not give a true picture of the price changes.

Now answer these questions:

1. What was the longest time period with no change in price?

2. If the line connecting points were solid, why do you think a reader might be confused about the price of a token?

Have you ever heard about prices for a train or bus fare dropping? What do you think happened?

Read the following story about the fight to drop token prices in Boston, MA.

> In 1981, the Massachusetts Bay Transit Authority (MBTA) raised subway fares. Many people started to drive instead of riding on public transit. The same year, a group called Conservation Law Foundation (CLF) sued the MBTA, claiming that the number of riders had decreased since the fares increased. The CLF lawyers argued that because the MBTA is an agency run in part with state monies, it should serve the people of Massachusetts. The cost of travel was too expensive for 10% or more of the people, and as a result they had stopped riding the subway. The MBTA said this was true, but not by as much as 10%, only by 9.9%. The judge sided with CLF and told the MBTA to stop charging so much. The MBTA complied by lowering the price of a subway ride to 60¢ for the next seven years.

Practice: National Park Visitors

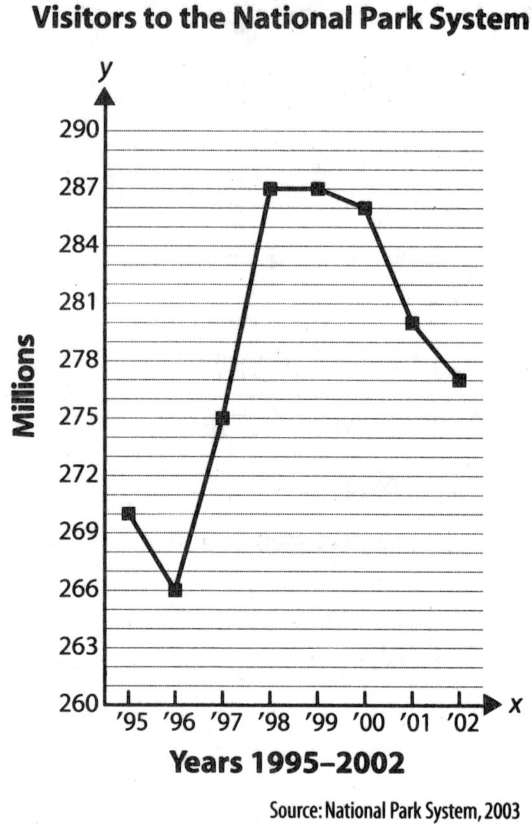

1. Describe what you see in the graph above.

2. Make two statements that are true descriptions or inferences based on the graph.

3. Make one statement that is a false description or inference based on the graph.

Practice: Salary History

Plot the data for Jerri's nonemployee compensation from Lovely Lawn and Landscaping over five years. Then answer the questions.

☐ CORRECTED (if checked)

PAYER'S name, street, address, city, state, and ZIP code	1 Rents	OMB No. 1545-0115	Miscellaneous Income
Lovely Lawn and Landscaping 353 Shady Lane Westport, ME 04578	$ 2 Royalties $	1999 Form 1099-MISC	
	3 Other income $	4 Federal income tax withheld $ 0.—	Copy B For Recipient
PAYER'S Federal identification number / RECIPIENT'S identification number	5 Fishing boat proceeds $	6 Medical and health care payments $	
RECIPIENT'S name Jerri XXX Street address (including apt. no.)	7 Nonemployee compensation $2,332.00	8 Substitute paymants in lieu of dividends of interest $	This is important tax information and is being furnished to the Internal Revenue Service. If you are

☐ CORRECTED (if checked)

PAYER'S name, street, address, city, state, and ZIP code	1 Rents	OMB No. 1545-0115	Miscellaneous Income
Lovely Lawn and Landscaping 353 Shady Lane Westport, ME 04578	$ 2 Royalties $	2000 Form 1099-MISC	
	3 Other income $	4 Federal income tax withheld $ 0.—	Copy B For Recipient
PAYER'S Federal identification number / RECIPIENT'S identification number	5 Fishing boat proceeds $	6 Medical and health care payments $	
RECIPIENT'S name Jerri XXX Street address (including apt. no.)	7 Nonemployee compensation $3,246.78	8 Substitute paymants in lieu of dividends of interest $	This is important tax information and is being furnished to the Internal Revenue Service. If you are

☐ CORRECTED (if checked)

PAYER'S name, street, address, city, state, and ZIP code	1 Rents	OMB No. 1545-0115	Miscellaneous Income
Lovely Lawn and Landscaping 353 Shady Lane Westport, ME 04578	$ 2 Royalties $	2001 Form 1099-MISC	
	3 Other income $	4 Federal income tax withheld $2,519.10	Copy B For Recipient
PAYER'S Federal identification number / RECIPIENT'S identification number	5 Fishing boat proceeds $	6 Medical and health care payments $	
RECIPIENT'S name Jerri XXX Street address (including apt. no.)	7 Nonemployee compensation $13,995.00	8 Substitute paymants in lieu of dividends of interest $	This is important tax information and is being furnished to the Internal Revenue Service. If you are

☐ CORRECTED (if checked)

PAYER'S name, street, address, city, state, and ZIP code		1 Rents	OMB No. 1545-0115	
Lovely Lawn and Landscaping 353 Shady Lane Westport, ME 04578		$	2002	Miscellaneous Income
		2 Royalties $	Form 1099-MISC	
		3 Other income $	4 Federal income tax withheld $ 0.—	Copy B For Recipient
PAYER'S Federal identification number	RECIPIENT'S identification number	5 Fishing boat proceeds $	6 Medical and health care payments $	
RECIPIENT'S name Jerri XXX		7 Nonemployee compensation $10,832.22	8 Substitute paymants in lieu of dividends of interest $	This is important tax information and is being furnished to the Internal Revenue Service. If you are
Street address (including apt. no.)				

☐ CORRECTED (if checked)

PAYER'S name, street, address, city, state, and ZIP code		1 Rents	OMB No. 1545-0115	
Lovely Lawn and Landscaping 353 Shady Lane Westport, ME 04578		$	2003	Miscellaneous Income
		2 Royalties $	Form 1099-MISC	
		3 Other income $	4 Federal income tax withheld $2,519.00	Copy B For Recipient
PAYER'S Federal identification number	RECIPIENT'S identification number	5 Fishing boat proceeds $	6 Medical and health care payments $	
RECIPIENT'S name Jerri XXX		7 Nonemployee compensation $13,995.00	8 Substitute paymants in lieu of dividends of interest $	This is important tax information and is being furnished to the Internal Revenue Service. If you are
Street address (including apt. no.)				

1. Between what years did the greatest change in Jerri's compensation occur?

2. When did her earnings more than double?

3. In __________ Jerri's earnings decreased by __________.

4. The most surprising thing about this graph is

5. Make up a story explaining why Jerri's income went up or down.

Practice: More Practice with Intervals

In the two graphs below, one number is given on each of the axes. Fill in the other numbers.

1\.

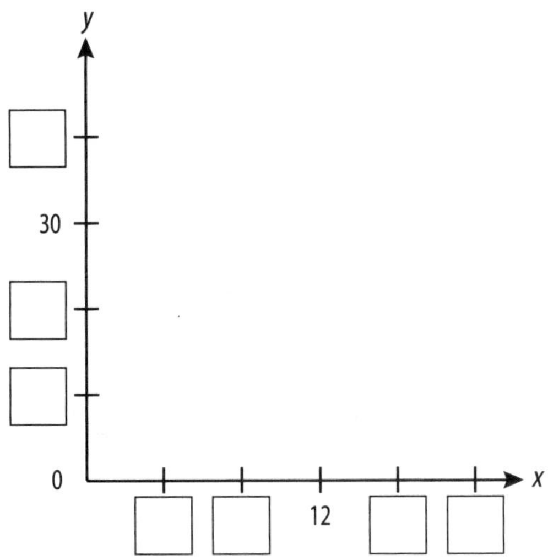

2\.

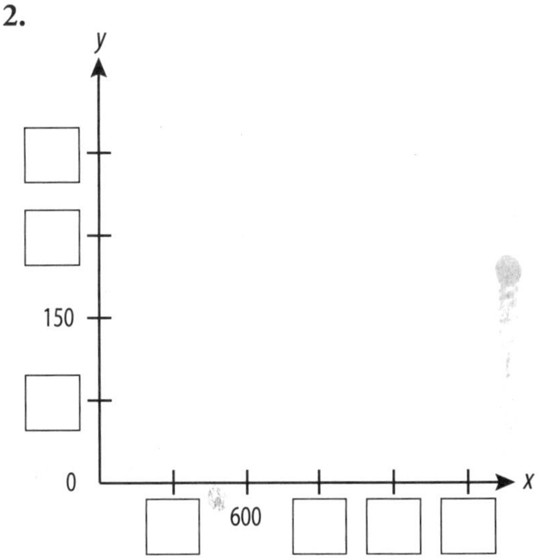

Check your answers. Start where the two axes meet, usually zero, and count by the numbers you have written in. Do they make sense? You can use this method when you try to figure out an unnumbered mark on a thermometer, stove dial, or other gauge.

3\.

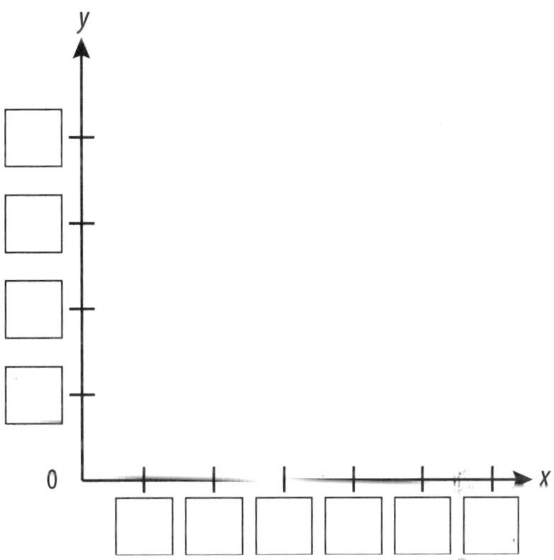

For Graph 3, write "$120" at the top of the *y*-axis. Then label the rest of the boxes on the *y*-axis. Fit the years 1990–2000 in the boxes given on the *x*-axis.

4.

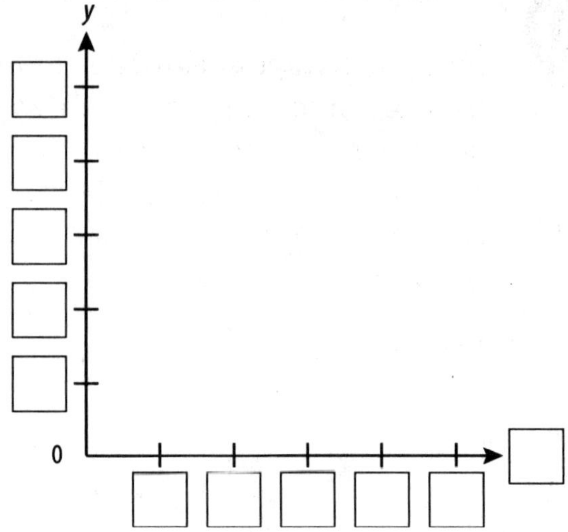

For Graph 4, write "100%" at the top of the y-axis. Then label the rest of the boxes on the y-axis. Fit the years 1980–2020 in the boxes given on the x-axis.

Extension: Dropping Below Zero

Line graphs can show amounts in negative numbers. For example, if a company loses more money than it makes, or if the temperature drops below zero, the line on a graph will drop too. Sometimes a positive number shows up on a graph as a negative number because it is below an expected amount. Negative numbers start near zero at –1 and continue, –2, –3, –4, –5, etc.

Example:

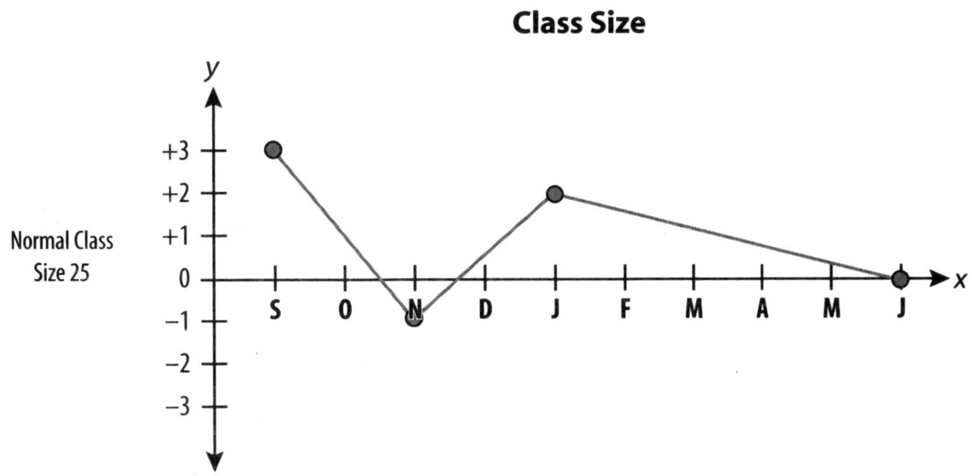

The normal size of first-grade classes is 25 children. In September 2000, the first grade had 28 students enrolled. In November, the number dropped to 24, but in January, three new students registered. In June, 25 students completed the first grade.

1. Complete the story.

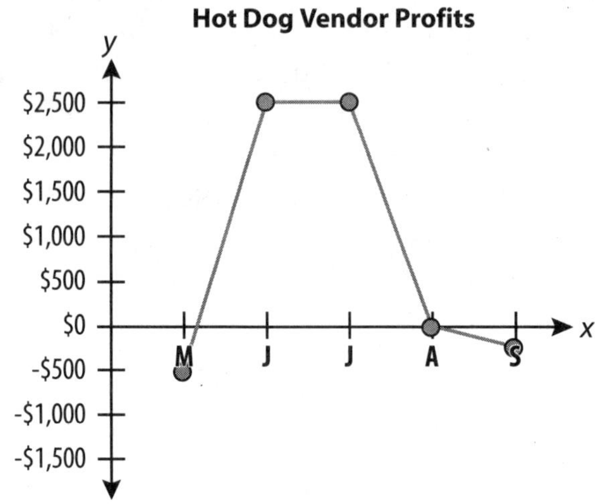

At the ballpark, a hot-dog vendor graphed his sales for one summer. In May, he lost $________ because he had more hot dogs on hand than he could sell. In June, the ballpark was sold out, and he made $________. In July, the profits stayed steady at $________. In August, he broke even, with ________ profit and zero loss. In September, he had a loss of $________.

2. Plot the points.

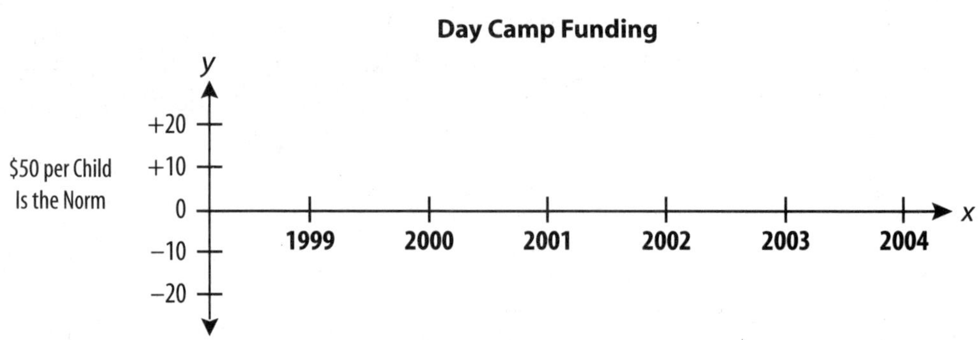

The local park funds its day camp based on the 1999 promised amount of $50 per child from the state. Make a graph to show the money coming from the state. A graph with negative numbers will show that there have been funding cuts. Use the $50 norm as the starting point, or equivalent of zero.

1999	$50 per child
2000	Level funding, $50 per child
2001	Funding increase to $65 per child
2002	Cut in funding to $45 per child
2003	Cut in funding to $30 per child

Test Practice

In the 1990s, many cellular telephone providers were not making money despite gaining new customers. They had to spend a lot of money to build their networks and attract new customers.

Below are two graphs that appeared in the *Chicago Tribune* in 2000, showing estimated total subscribers and their average monthly bills over a period of several years.

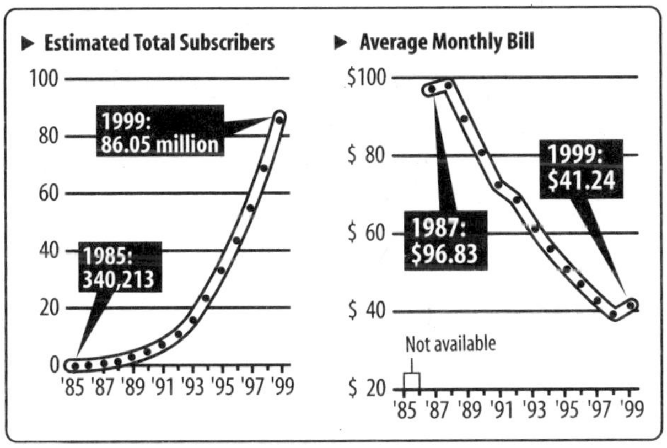

Source: Wow.com Chicago Tribune © 2000 KRT

Items 1–3 refer to the graphs. Choose the answer that best describes the information in the graphs.

1. Which of the following best describes the estimated total subscribers for wireless telephone?
   (1) The total subscribers increased most between 1985 and 1991.
   (2) The total subscribers increased most between 1991 and 1997.
   (3) The total subscribers decreased most between 1991 and 1997.
   (4) The total subscribers decreased steadily between 1985 and 1999.
   (5) The total subscribers increased more between 1985 and 1991 than between 1989 and 1993.

2. Based on the graphs, which of the following statements is true?
   (1) There is no relationship between total number of subscribers and average cost of monthly service.
   (2) The monthly cost of using cellular telephones has continued to increase despite the total number of subscribers.
   (3) As the total number of subscribers increased, the monthly cost to subscribers increased.
   (4) As the total number of subscribers increased, the monthly cost to subscribers decreased.
   (5) As the monthly cost of service declined, the number of subscribers also declined.

3. According to the graph, which of the following statements about the average monthly bill for cellular telephones is true?
   (1) The average monthly bill has increased by $254 since 1985.
   (2) The average monthly bill has increased by $20 between 1998 and 1999.
   (3) The average monthly bill has doubled since 1987.
   (4) The average monthly bill has decreased by about 25% since 1987.
   (5) The average monthly bill is about half what it was in 1987.

Items 4–6 are based on the line graph below, which shows visitors to the national park system.

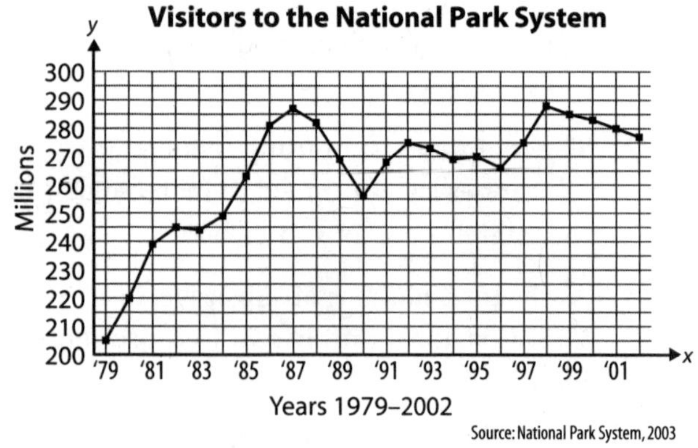

4. During which time period did the largest increase in visitors occur?

(1) 1979–1982

(2) 1983–1985

(3) 1990–1992

(4) 1992–1994

(5) 1996–1998

5. During which time period did the number of visitors decline for four years in a row?

(1) 1979–1982

(2) 1989–1992

(3) 1993–1996

(4) 1986–1990

(5) 1998–2001

6. Based on the graph, about how many million more visitors were there to national parks in 1990 than in 1983?

LESSON **7**

A Mean Idea

How many hours on average do you watch TV?

In this lesson, you will focus on the idea of **average**. You have heard the word "average" used in many situations: batting average, average weight and height for children, and average price of gasoline, for example. What do you think of when you hear the word "average"?

You will use different strategies to figure out the average. You will define, predict, calculate, and graph one average, the **mean,** for several data sets.

Americans watch so much TV!

Lola: "You know I come from Jamaica, and now I live with and work for an American family. I am surprised. Americans watch so much TV!"

Joanne: "You cannot base your idea of America on just one family."

Lola: "I see it. They watch from afternoon until bedtime. That is six hours a day for the children."

Joanne: "Do they watch TV more on some days and less on others? In the summer the children might watch less TV. One study I read said that the average American watches three hours of TV a day."

Lola: "That tells me nothing. An average is not a real person. I have seen real people in their own home."

Questions: What point is Lola trying to make? How do people find averages?

Activity 1: The TV Is On

1. Find the average using Post-it Notes or pennies.

Jess		Al	
Monday	2 hours	Sunday	10 hours
Tuesday	2 hours	Monday	5 hours
Wednesday	4 hours	Tuesday	4 hours
Thursday	2 hours	Wednesday	2 hours
Friday	5 hours	Thursday	4 hours

2. Find the average on a calculator.

3. Make a graph showing Al's TV-watching hours.

4. Describe the data set:

Jess watched TV for __________ days. The fewest number of hours she watched in a single day was __________. The highest number of hours she watched in one day was __________. The mean number of hours per day of watching TV for Jess was __________. Al watched TV for __________ days. The fewest number of hours he watched in a single day was __________. The highest number of hours he watched in one day was __________. The mean number of hours per day of watching TV for Al was __________.

Activity 2: A Mean Score

Polly, Molly, and Dolly are in a class where each student's final grade is determined by an average of all his or her grades for the semester: five tests and the final exam.

Polly's Test Scores, fall:
85, 88, 90, 88, 78, 92

Polly's Test Scores, spring:
91, 90, 95, 78, 82, _____
target average: 86

Molly's Test Scores, fall:
100, 98, 90, 93, 83, 85

Molly's Test Scores, spring:
79, 85, 74, 68, 79, _____
target average: 76

Dolly's Test Scores, fall:
80, 74, 86, 90, 91, 89

Dolly's Test Scores, spring:
92, 96, 100, 96, 92, _____
target average: 93

Wally's GED scores*:
Social Studies 440, Science 410, Literature 500, Mathematics 410, Writing 420

Wally's GED Retest Plan:
Social Studies, Science, Literature, Mathematics, Writing

Holly's GED scores:
Social Studies 430, Science 410, Literature 410, Mathematics 410, Writing 450

Holly's GED Retest scores:
Social Studies 450, Science 480, Literature 410, Mathematics 440, Writing 450

*To pass the General Education Development (GED) test, the following scores are required: 2,250 the minimum total, 450 the mean, 410 the minimum on any one test.

For each round, use a different method to show your work and check your answers.

Round 1

Predict the mean scores for Polly, Molly, and Dolly in the fall semester.

Find the mean scores for Polly, Molly, and Dolly in the fall semester.

Make notes about the data set. Include the lowest, highest, and mean scores.

Round 2

Predict the mean score on the GED test for Wally and Holly.

Find the mean score on the GED test for Wally and Holly.

Make notes about the data set. Include the lowest, highest, and mean scores.

Round 3

What is the lowest score Polly, Molly, and Dolly can each get on her final exam in the spring to make her target average?

Predict

Polly: Final exam grade ________ Final average ________

Molly: Final exam grade ________ Final average ________

Dolly: Final exam grade ________ Final average ________

Actual

Polly: Final exam grade ________ Final average ________

Molly: Final exam grade ________ Final average ________

Dolly: Final exam grade ________ Final average ________

Round 4

Wally plans to retest in one area. How many points higher must he score on that test to pass with a total score of 2,250?

Holly has taken three tests over again. What is her new average? Does she pass now?

Practice: Mental Mean

1. Find the average of the numbers using mental math. Look for patterns.

		Mean
Ages	5 and 10	
Lottery ticket prices	$5 and $10	
Miles traveled	50 and 100	
Number of students	500 and 1,000	
Scholarship amounts	$5,000 and $10,000	
Building project bids	$5 million and $10 million	

2. Find the average of the numbers using mental math. Look for patterns.

		Mean
Ages	52 and 62	
Miles traveled	520 and 620	
Number of students	5,200 and 6,200	
Scholarship amounts	$52,000 and $62,000	
Building project bids	$5.2 million and $6.2 million	

3. Find the average of the numbers using mental math. Look for patterns. Combine pairs of numbers to make adding easier. Check your work.

	Set 1	Mean	Set 2	Mean
Ages	3, 5, 7, and 9		18, 24, 32, and 36	
Lottery winnings	$30, $50, $70, and $90		$180, $240, $320, and $360	
Miles traveled	300, 500, 700, and 900		1,800, 2,400, 3,200, and 3,600	
Project bids	$3,000, $5,000, $7,000, and $9,000		$18,000, $24,000, $32,000, and $36,000	

Practice: Among Friends

1. Ella had $7.00 in her pocket. She asked her six friends how much pocket money they had.

$2.15	$2.00	$4.50
$5.65	$20.00	$0

   a. The average of everyone's pocket money is ______________.

   b. Is there enough money for each person to get a bagel and coffee for $2.25 apiece if they don't stop at a bank?

   c. Could they all go to a movie for $8.00 per person?

   d. To find the average, Ella totaled and divided by ______________.

2. The Sunshine Day Care Center measured the 12 four-year-olds that attend the center. Graph the children's heights.

   The mean height to the nearest inch for these four-year-olds is ____________.

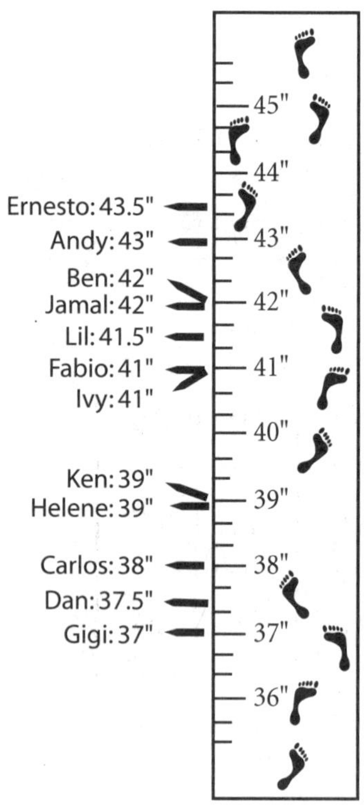

Number the *y*-axis every 2 inches starting at 36 inches.

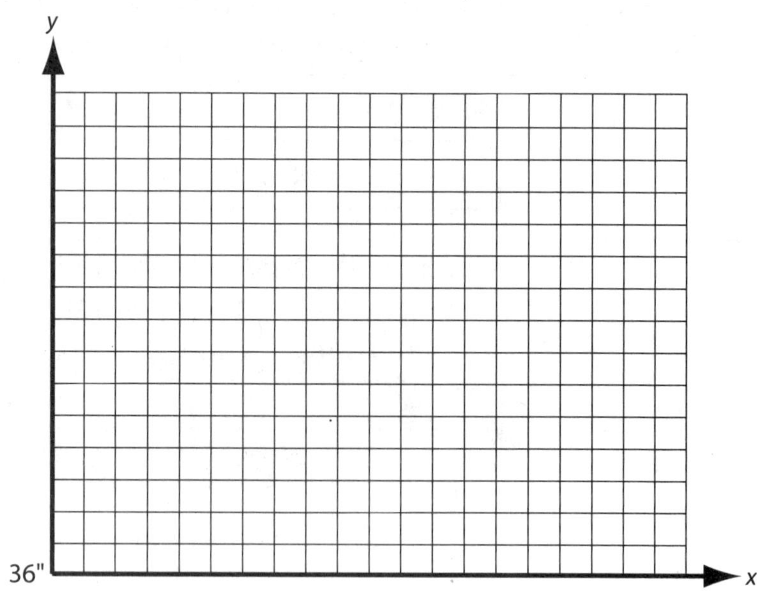

   a. Carlos's brothers call him a shrimp, but in fact he is only ______ inches shorter than the mean height for four-year-olds, as established in the class.

   b. Ivy's parents call her a big girl. At four, she is _______ inches taller than the mean height for children her age.

Practice: Data Collection

1. Check your newspaper or the Internet, or listen to the weather report on the radio or TV for data on temperatures.

2. Find the high and low temperatures predicted for five consecutive days.

3. Write the data in the table.

Date					
Temperature					

4. Bring this information to class.

Extension: The Nurse's Mean

1. Mari's school may cut her school nurse job to save money. She keeps a record for four weeks of the children she sees. Students come to her office every day, and sometimes she goes to classes to give health talks.

	M	T	W	T	F
Week 1	15	11	11	19	34
Week 2	21	15	8	44	47
Week 3	10	16	9	25	20
Week 4	26	18	12	30	39

a. Describe Mari's week. Which are her busiest days? Which are her slowest days?

b. What is the average number of children she sees per day?

c. If Mari needed to attend a meeting, which day would be least likely to interfere with her work in school?

d. Which week should she report when she defends her job?

e. Which statistic do you think will make a stronger case, an average day or an average week?

2. Imagine that before going in for a surgical procedure, the doctor tells you that you will be able to work again after three days. A friend who is a nurse says the average recuperation time for a person your age is three weeks. How might you use that information to make plans for coverage at work and extra childcare?

Some things to think about:

Are you in better health than average or not?

Do you recover faster than average or not?

Explain your plan. Explain your reasons.

Test Practice

Item 1 refers to the following table:

	Milk	Chips	Butter	Eggs	Ice Cream
Corner Store	$3.29	$1.25	$5.29	$2.49	$3.99
Super-market	$3.09	$0.89	$3.99	$1.45	$3.29

1. An informal survey confirmed that corner stores are more expensive places to shop than supermarkets. Based on the information in the table, *on average*, how much more does a person pay per item at a corner store for the items listed?

   (1) $0.72

   (2) $2.54

   (3) $3.60

   (4) $3.09

   (5) $3.29

Items 2–4 refer to this table:

National Park Service Sites	Number of Recreational Visitors, 2002 (in millions)
Blue Ridge Parkway	21.5
Franklin Delano Roosevelt Memorial	2.5
Golden Gate	13.9
Grand Canyon	4.0
Great Smoky Mountains	9.3
Indiana Dunes	1.9
Lake Mead	7.5
Statue of Liberty	3.4
Yellowstone	2.9

Source: National Park Service, 2003

2. The National Parks Director wants less visited tourist attractions to increase their visitor numbers to the mean for all the national parks. These less visited parks say the mean is not fair because the Blue Ridge Parkway spans two states and accounts for a large number of visitors. They argue that a mean found without the Blue Ridge Parkway would be more realistic. Excluding the Blue Ridge Parkway, what would be the approximate mean number of recreational visitors to national parks in 2002?

   (1) 4.87 million

   (2) 5.68 million

   (3) 7.26 million

   (4) 43.8 million

   (5) 65.3 million

3. If the Blue Ridge Parkway were counted as two national parks instead of one, what would have been the average number of recreational visitors to national parks in 2002?

   (1) 6.69 million

   (2) 9.26 million

   (3) 10.75 million

   (4) 32.65 million

   (5) 65.3 million

4. If the Blue Ridge Parkway were still counted as one national park, which of the following would be true about the mean number of recreational visitors to national parks in 2002?

   (1) The mean would be higher than the number of visitors to Lake Mead National Park.

   (2) The mean would be higher than the number of visitors to Grand Canyon National Park.

   (3) The mean would be lower than the number of visitors to the Statue of Liberty.

   (4) The mean would be 2.9 million.

   (5) The mean would be 7.25 million.

5. An adult education class conducted an informal poll on time spent waiting in line for rides at a major amusement park. Below are the results of their survey. What is the average wait time during these holidays, according to their data?

   (1) 1 hour, 21 minutes

   (2) 1 hour, 25 minutes

   (3) 1 hour, 38 minutes

   (4) 8 hours, 13 minutes

   (5) 82 hours, 33 minutes

Holiday	Wait Time (in minutes)
New Year's Day	100
Presidents Day	58
Fourth of July	107
Columbus Day	60
Thanksgiving	80

6. Jake's household consists of his father and himself. Three people live in the house next door. The number found by averaging the size of the two households is the same as the number for the average size of households in the United States. Write the number for the average U.S. household size to the nearest tenth.

LESSON **8**

Mystery Cities

What about this graph is different from graphs you have seen in class?

In this lesson, you will examine graphs that show two different types of information at once. You will compare graphs and stories about weather. As you look at different graphs, you will be asked to describe the weather stories they show.

Comparing a graph and a story helps you decide what to believe. Ask yourself: Do the graph and story make sense together? Or does the graph indicate one trend and the story another? Trace the story of the graph. Then pick out key information from the graph and the story to compare.

Climate graphs give you a chance to handle two kinds of information at a time.

Where does average temperature data come from? Every major city has one or more weather stations, mostly located at airports where skyscrapers will not block rainfall. If weather data are collected by a machine, the temperature and **precipitation** are checked hourly. If people collect the data, they check once or twice a day. Weather scientists, or meteorologists, then find and record the averages.

Activity 1: Reading Climate Graphs

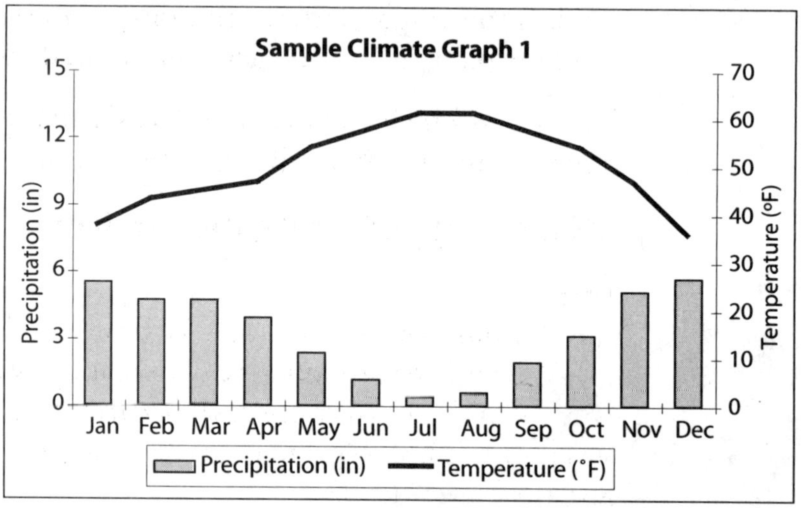

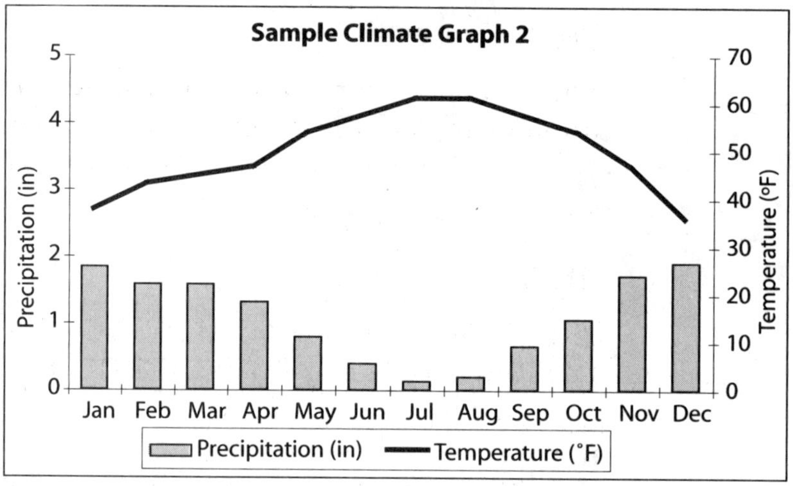

1. How are the two climate graphs alike?

2. How are the two climate graphs different?

3. Take a reading and record the data for February for each graph:

	Climate Graph 1	Climate Graph 2
Temperature	____________	____________
Precipitation	____________	____________

4. Notes:

Activity 2: Mystery Cities

Look at the graphs and descriptions of cities on the following pages. Find the pictures and the descriptions that go together.

Now guess which city each graph and story describe. (*Hint*: Each city is a large city in the United States. Four cities are on coasts.)

Mystery Cities Climate Descriptions

City 1

It is dry most of the time. The daytime temperatures in July can easily be over 100°F. Even at night, the temperature is warm, in the 80s. The winters in this city are crisp, with warm days and cool nights. In the summer it is hot. Most people who want to visit plan to come in the fall and spring.

City 2

People who live here enjoy warm temperatures year round. The summers are humid, with thunderstorms and heavy rain. Heavy rains can also occur in the spring and especially in the fall when hurricanes blow through the state.

City 3

This city has the same weather year round: blue skies, little rain, and mild temperatures (in the 70s). Extreme heat or cold in this city is rare.

City 4

This city usually has the same amount of precipitation every month—summer, spring, winter, and fall. Despite the similarity in precipitation, winter and summer have extremely different temperatures. June, July, and August are hot and humid.

City 5

The temperatures in this city never go too high or too low; the summers are not too hot and the winters are not freezing cold. Most of the rain falls between November and April; the driest months are in the summer.

Mystery Cities' Climate Graphs

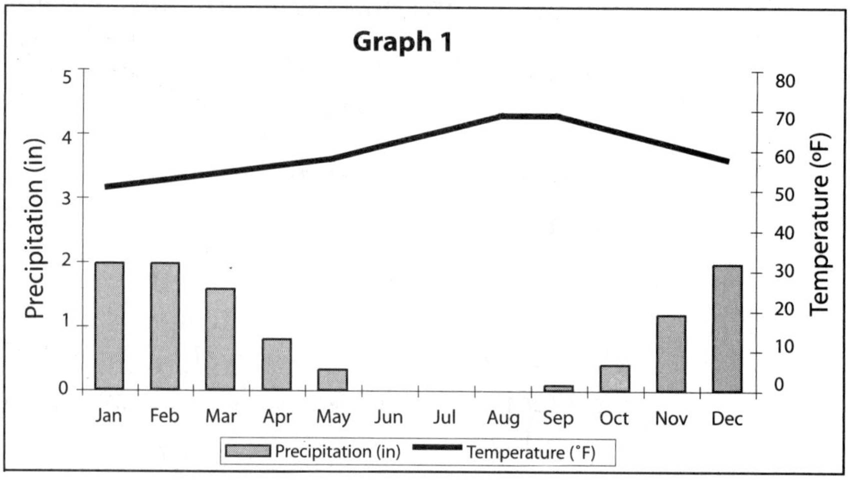

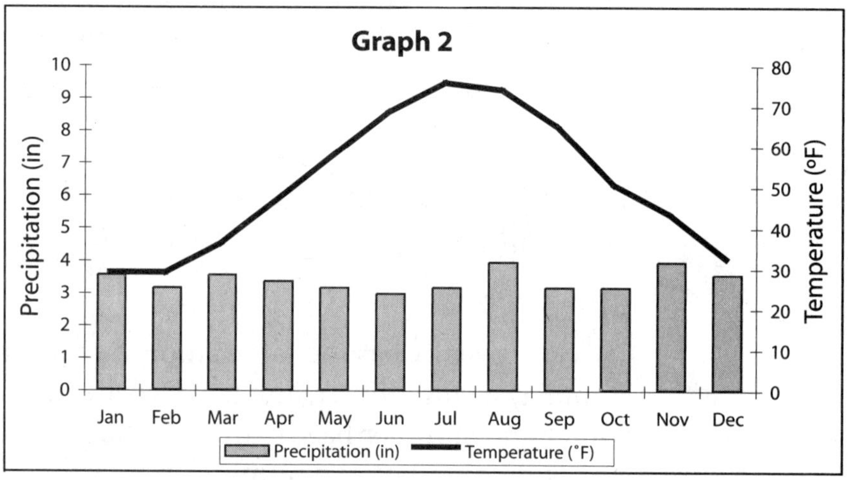

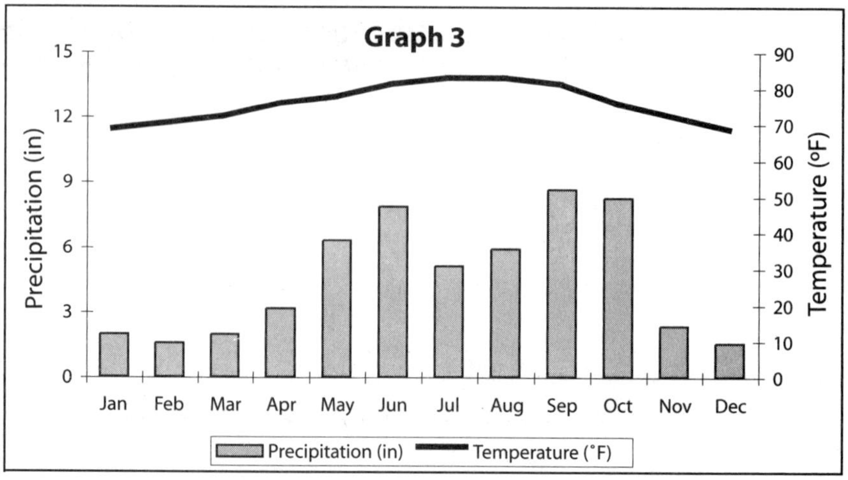

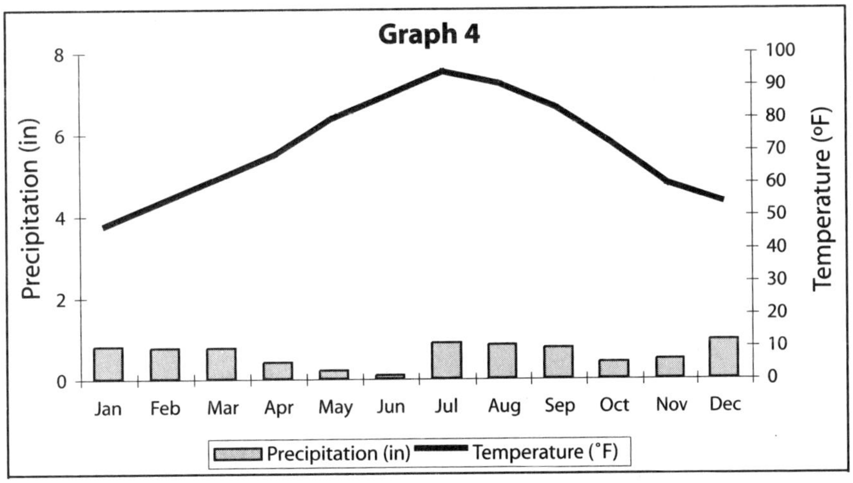

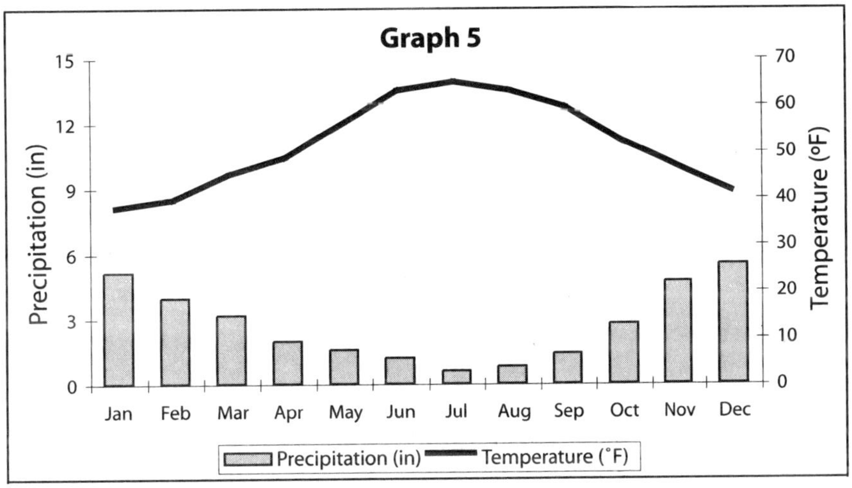

If you have difficulty reading graphs with two sets of information, try this:

- Make sure you have two extra copies of the graph.
- Highlight the line on one of the graphs with a colored marker so it really stands out for you.
- Now read just the line graph and make notes about what you see.
- On the other graph, with a different colored marker, highlight the tops of each bar on the graph.
- Read the graph and jot down what you notice about the bars.

Practice: Incomplete Climate Graphs!

The climate graphs below were started but never finished. Complete the graphs using the data given. You will have to estimate. Use what you have learned about inferring numbers when reading the lines of a thermometer or a ruler.

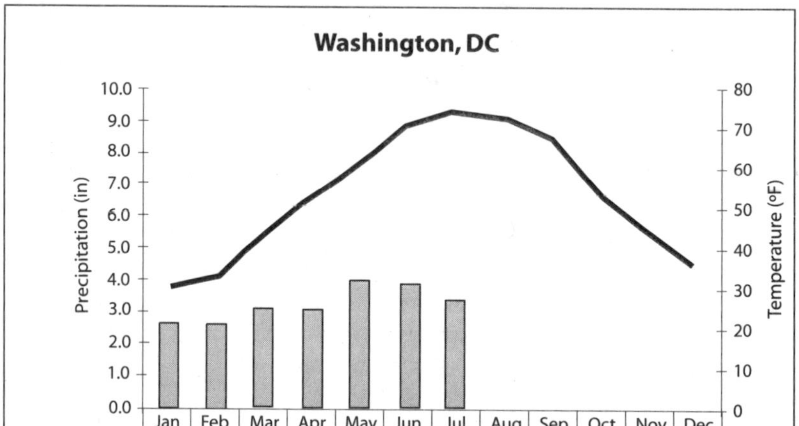

	Jan	Feb	Mar	Apr	May	Jun	Jul	Aug	Sep	Oct	Nov	Dec
Prec (in)	2.7	2.7	3.1	3.0	4.0	3.9	3.5	4.0	3.3	3.2	3.1	3.1
Temp (ºF)	30	34	45	54	63	72	75	73	68	54	45	36

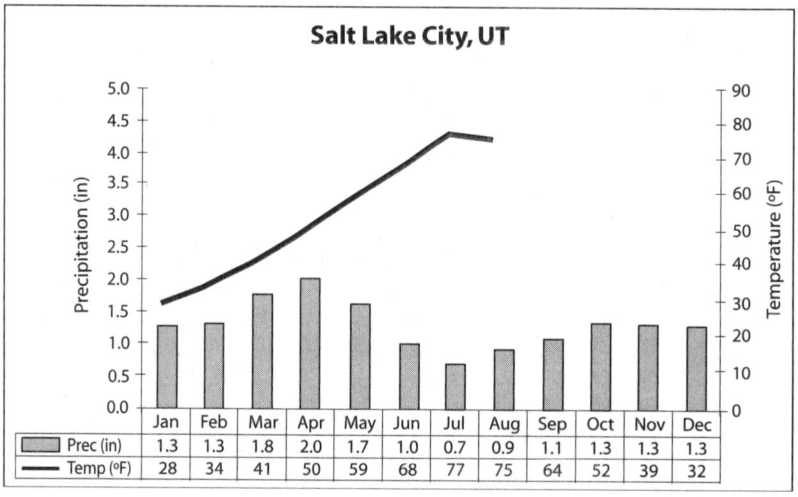

	Jan	Feb	Mar	Apr	May	Jun	Jul	Aug	Sep	Oct	Nov	Dec
Prec (in)	1.3	1.3	1.8	2.0	1.7	1.0	0.7	0.9	1.1	1.3	1.3	1.3
Temp (ºF)	28	34	41	50	59	68	77	75	64	52	39	32

Denver, CO

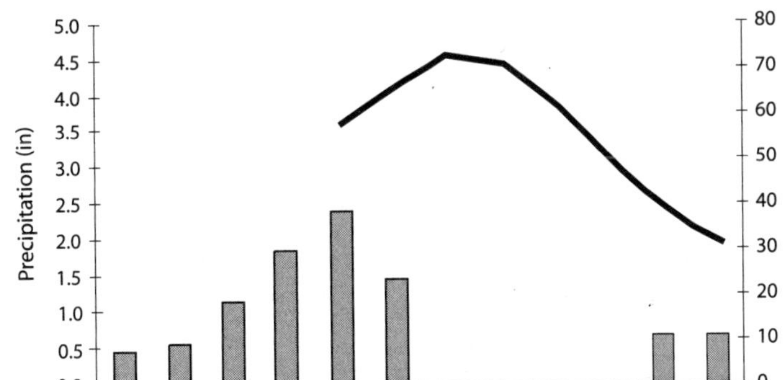

	Jan	Feb	Mar	Apr	May	Jun	Jul	Aug	Sep	Oct	Nov	Dec
Prec (in)	0.4	0.5	1.1	1.9	2.4	1.4	1.7	1.5	1.0	1.0	0.7	0.7
Temp (ºF)	30	32	39	48	57	66	73	72	63	50	39	32

Detroit, MI

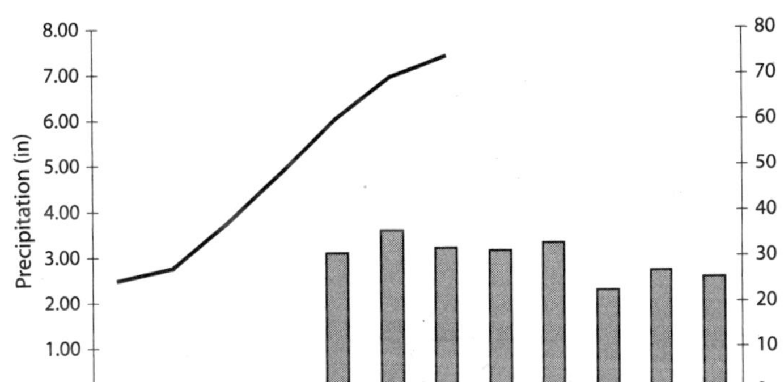

	Jan	Feb	Mar	Apr	May	Jun	Jul	Aug	Sep	Oct	Nov	Dec
Prec (in)	1.91	1.88	2.52	3.05	3.05	3.55	3.16	3.10	3.27	2.23	2.66	2.51
Temp (ºF)	24.5	27.2	36.9	48.1	59.8	69.0	73.5	71.8	63.9	51.9	40.7	29.6

Extension: Quality of Life 1

You are in the process of moving to San Diego, CA. You have narrowed your choice of apartments to two in a suburb called Mission Beach.

Apt. 1	Apt. 2
MISSION BEACH FOR RENT: 2BR $650 W/D, AC, off-street parking in a quiet neighborhood. 672 Park St. 619-555-6908	**MISSION BEACH** FOR RENT: 2BR $750 W/D, AC, patio, off-street parking, utilities included. 851 Shell St. 619-555-6908

The rent for the first apartment does not include the cost of heating and air conditioning. The rent for the second apartment does. To estimate how much your energy bills will be, you asked a friend who lives in downtown San Diego to send a copy of her energy bills from last year.

The table shows her utility costs for the first six months.

Month	Utility Cost	Cost of Apt. 1	Cost of Apt. 2
Jan	$75		
Feb	$72		
Mar	$60		
Apr	$60		
May	$50		
Jun	$70		

Draw the two different monthly apartment rental costs on one graph to show which has the lower average monthly rent. Be sure to label the axes.

> You might find it helpful to complete the table before you make the graph.

Extension: Quality of Life 2

Your brother-in-law enjoys cooking out. He claims that when he lived in Phoenix he grilled outside all the time. Now that he lives in Seattle, he complains that he cannot cook out as often.

The table below shows the number of times he actually grilled outside in each place.

	Cooked Out	
	Phoenix	**Seattle**
Jan	0	0
Feb	0	0
Mar	8	0
Apr	20	0
May	20	10
Jun	5	25
Jul	0	28
Aug	0	25
Sep	22	25
Oct	22	16
Nov	22	0
Dec	22	0

Make one graph that compares the two sets of information.

How does the data from the graph compare to what your brother-in-law claimed?

Explain why the two sets of data have different trends. Use the climate graphs for Phoenix and Seattle to help with your explanation.

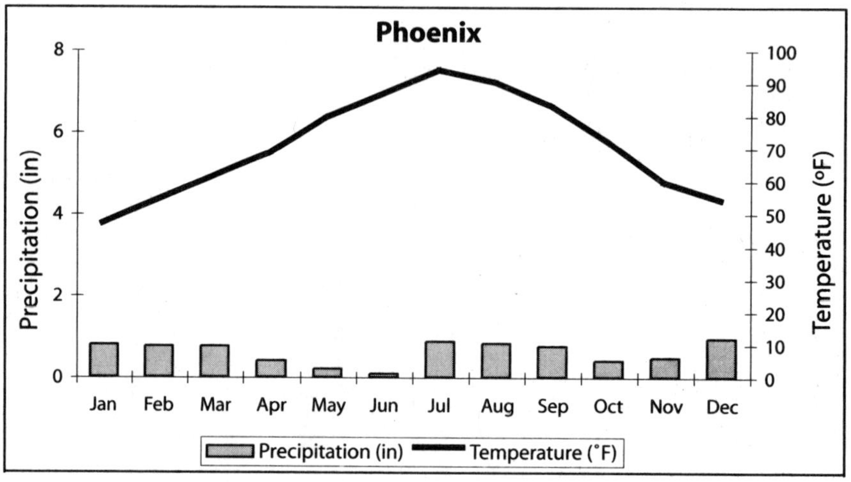

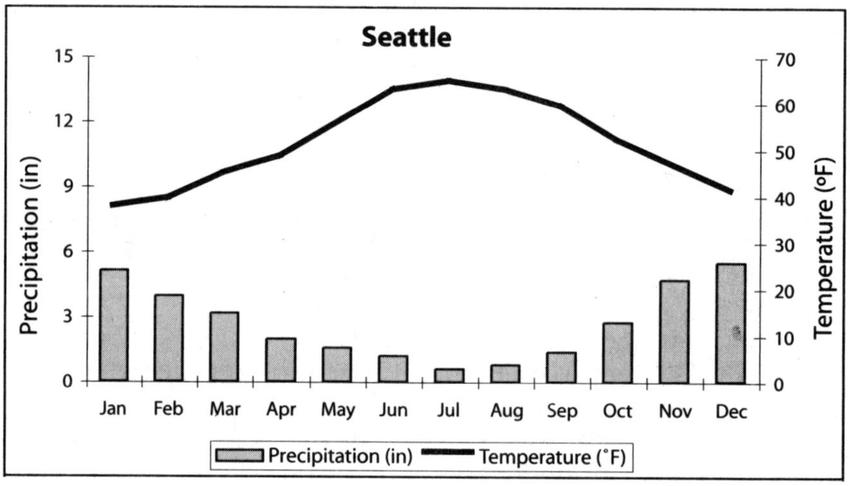

Test Practice

Question 1 is based on "Sample Climate Graph 1."

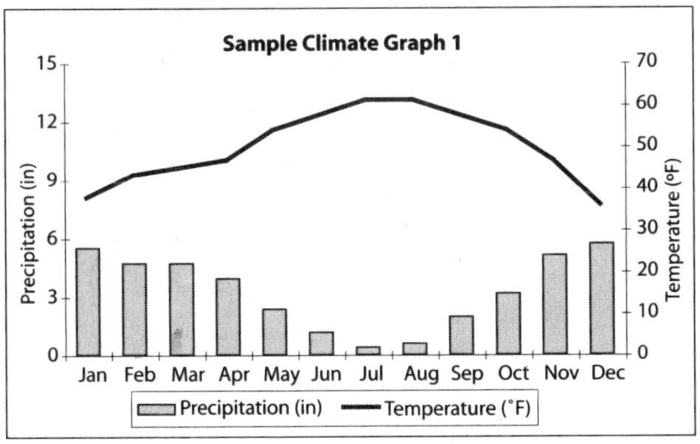

1. Which statement is true, according to this graph?
   (1) The summer is mild and it rains a lot.
   (2) The summer is mild and it rains very little.
   (3) The summer is very hot and there is very little rain.
   (4) The winter is very cold (below freezing) and there is little rain.
   (5) The winter is very cold (below freezing) and there is a lot of rain.

Question 2 is based on this climate graph of Phoenix.

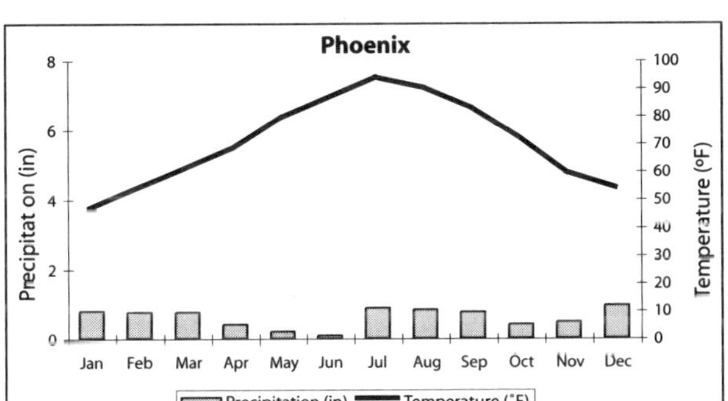

2. According to the graph, this city would probably have
   (1) Winter sports such as cross-country skiing available.
   (2) Lots of desert-like vegetation.
   (3) Very cold summers.
   (4) Drought-like conditions in the spring.
   (5) Drought-like conditions in the winter.

Questions 3 and 4 refer to "Unemployment Rate: 1990–2000."

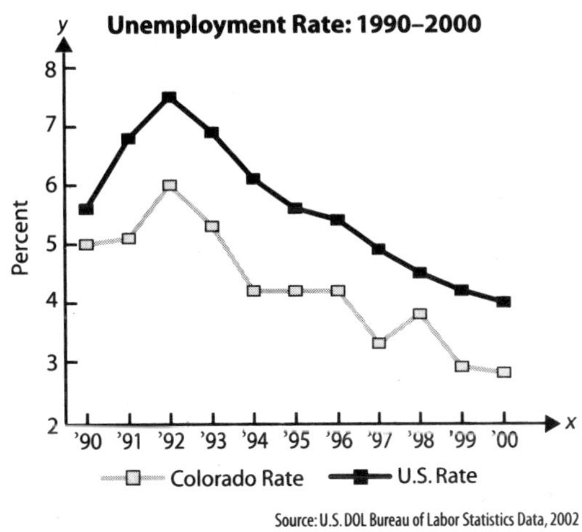

3. Ping was considering moving to Denver and wondered how Colorado's unemployment rate compared to the national average. Based on the graph, what general statement could she make?
   (1) There are fewer people unemployed in Colorado than in any other state.
   (2) The unemployment rate for Colorado has decreased every year from 1990 to 2000.
   (3) The unemployment rate for the United States has decreased every year from 1990 to 2000.
   (4) The national unemployment rate is lower than Colorado's.
   (5) The national unemployment rate is higher than Colorado's.

4. According to the graph, which of the following statements is true?

   (1) The United States and Colorado had increases in unemployment rates in 1992.

   (2) Both the United States and Colorado had decreases in unemployment rates from 1993 to 2000.

   (3) In 1991, the U.S. unemployment rate was almost double Colorado's rate.

   (4) In 1999, Colorado had about 100 fewer people unemployed than the United States.

   (5) There were more people unemployed in Colorado in 1990 than in the United States in 1997.

Questions 5 and 6 refer to this graph about occupational injuries.

Fatal Occupational Injuries 1990–2000
Logging vs. Grocery Store Work

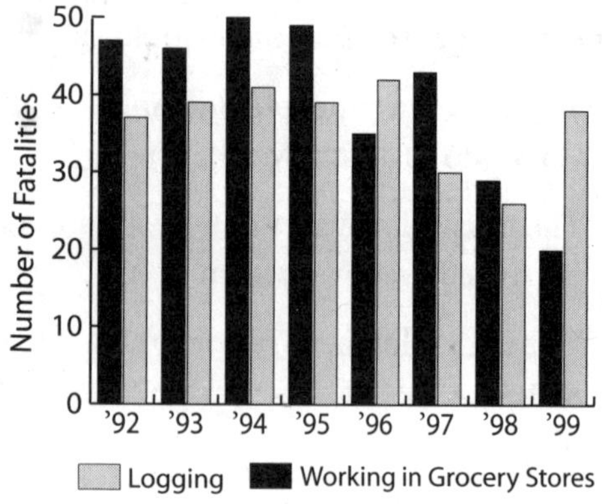

Source: U.S. DOL, Bureau of Labor Statistics Data, 2002

5. What might account for the fact that there were more deaths working in grocery stores than in logging between the years 1992 and 1999, as reported in the graph?

   (1) Grocery stores are more dangerous places to work.

   (2) Loggers are more careful than grocery-store employees.

   (3) Many more people work in grocery stores than in the logging industry.

   (4) Grocery-store managers do not care about safety.

   (5) Most loggers wear protective clothing.

6. According to the graph above, in which year were there almost twice as many fatalities in the logging industry as in the grocery store industry?

LESSON **9**

Median

Who represents the median height?

In this lesson, you will learn about another description for a "center" of a set of data. Like the median strip that divides a highway, the **median** is the middle point of a data set. When you hear, "The median is ...," you know that half the data points are above the median and half are below.

Do you know the median height of the people in your class? You will figure it out in class as you line up. You will also find the median for sets of data with even and odd numbers of items.

Activity 1: Line Up

1. ____________________ represents the median height of our class.
(name)

2. The median height of our class is ____________________.

3. Half the people are taller than ____________________.

4. Half the people are shorter than ____________________.

5. The heights range from ____________________ to
(height of shortest person)

____________________.
(height of tallest person)

Activity 2: At the Party

Invent eight or more ages for a data set that match the median and the story.

Story 1

The median age was 16; there were lots of moms and kids.

Story 2

At 27, I was the oldest person at the party; the median age was 17.

Story 3

The median age was 18; there were several grandchildren and their grandparents.

Story 4

Most of the attendees came to the party by van. Overall, it looked like the median age of the partygoers was 75.

Practice: Finding the Median

In each problem, find the median.

1. The test scores in Mr. Larson's tenth-grade English class were as follows:

   85 96 72 77 98 50 80 81 76 74 85

   What was the median score?

2. In 1980, the monthly prices of a dozen large Grade A eggs were

Jan: $0.88	Feb: $0.77	Mar: $0.81	Apr: $0.80
May: $0.74	Jun: $0.73	Jul: $0.78	Aug: $0.91
Sept: $0.90	Oct: $0.87	Nov: $0.92	Dec: $1.03

Source: U.S. DOL Bureau of Labor Statistics, http://www.bls.gov, 2004

   What was the median monthly price of a dozen large Grade A eggs in 1980?

3. At South High School, 10 sophomore boys were complaining about their heights. What is the median height of this group?

Andre: 63 inches	Fred: 64 inches
Ben: 72 inches	Gabriel: 66 inches
Colin: 70 inches	Hector: 63 inches
David: 65 inches	Ian: 65 inches
Ethan: 64 inches	Juan: 64 inches

A chart created by the National Center for Health Statistics shows the average height for boys this age to be a little over 5-$\frac{1}{2}$ feet. Do you think these tenth-graders should be worried? Why?
(*Hint*: 1 foot = 12 inches.)

Extension: The Average Wage

The weekly wages for the nine staff members at the M&M Inn are shown in the following table:

Job Category	Payroll Checks	Weekly Wage
Cook/Baker		$500
Housekeeper		$400
Office Manager	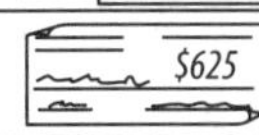	$625
Grounds/Building Maintenance		$550
Owner	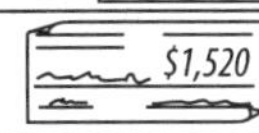	$1,520

1. What is the median weekly wage for the staff at the M&M Inn?

2. What is the mean weekly wage for the staff at the M&M Inn?

3. What does the mean tell you?

4. What does the median tell you?

5. You are a baker at the M&M Inn, and you think your salary is too low. Which average would you use to argue your point? Why?

Extension: Mean or Median?

For each of the following scenarios, determine which measure of center you think would best describe the center of the data set: the mean or the median.

1. The monthly rental fee for nine two-bedroom apartments:

$850	$950	$750
$650	$700	$675
$775	$1,200	$825

What is the median? ________ What is the mean? ________

Which best describes the center of the data? ________Why?

2. The time spent on phone calls by ten 12-year-olds:

20 min.	13 min.	5 min.	45 min.	35 min.
25 min.	18 min.	30 min.	3 min.	2 hours

What is the median? ________ What is the mean? ________

Which best describes the center of the data? ________Why?

3. The miles run per runner per week for a group of 11 runners:

5 miles	7 miles	14 miles	14 miles	25 miles
28 miles	34 miles	32 miles	10 miles	27 miles
8 miles				

What is the median? ________ What is the mean? _______

Which best describes the center of the data? _______Why?

4. The weekly salaries of six truck drivers:

$200	$180	$500
$220	$250	$275

What is the median? ________ What is the mean? _______

Which best describes the center of the data? _______Why?

Test Practice

1. Carlos said that the median income for his family is $15,000. Which of the following data sets could represent his family's median income?
   (1) Father: $21,000, Mother: $13,000, Uncle: $12,000, Carlos: $14,000
   (2) Father: $14,000, Mother: $16,000, Uncle: $17,000, Carlos: $16,000
   (3) Father: $14,000, Mother: $14,000, Uncle: $16,000, Carlos: $14,000
   (4) Father: $15,000, Mother: $12,000, Uncle: $17,000, Carlos: $20,000
   (5) Father: $14,000, Mother: $13,000, Uncle: $16,000, Carlos: $20,000

Items 2 and 3 refer to the data shown below on approximate mileage covered by some of the world's largest subway systems.

Moscow:	204	St. Petersburg:	66
Mexico City:	121	Osaka:	68
London:	249	Hong Kong:	49
New York City:	223	Paris:	127

2. What is the approximate median length in miles covered by the subway systems?
   (1) 121 miles
   (2) 124 miles
   (3) 127 miles
   (4) 138.875 miles
   (5) 200 miles

3. Which of the cities has a system that is approximately double the median length in miles?
   (1) Moscow
   (2) Mexico City
   (3) Paris
   (4) London
   (5) St. Petersburg

4. In 2000, the U.S. Department of Justice published data on the number of adults incarcerated in various states in the Southwest. Based on the available data, what is the median number of adults incarcerated in the Southwest?

State	Adults Incarcerated
AZ	101,100
NM	22,700
OK	61,400
TX	755,700

Source: U.S. Department of Justice, 2000

   (1) 235,225
   (2) 42,050
   (3) 61,400
   (4) 81,250
   (5) 101,100

5. Refer to the table in Question 4. If Colorado, which has 70,600 incarcerated adults, were added to the states listed in the Southwest region, how would that impact the median number?

   (1) It would raise the median number by about 10,000.

   (2) It would raise the median number by about 20,000.

   (3) It would lower the median number by about 10,000.

   (4) It would lower the median number by about 20,000.

   (5) It would not impact the median number of incarcerated adults at all.

6. Zookeepers have been keeping data on when baby deer begin to eat solid food. Based on the data they collected (shown below), what would they say the median age is at which deer begin to eat solid food?

   Deer A: 2 months

   Deer B: 5 weeks

   Deer C: 9 weeks

   Deer D: 1 month, 3 days

   Deer X: 49 days

   Deer Y: 35 days

LESSON **10**

Stock Prices

What statistics are used to describe stock prices?

This lesson focuses on the **stock market**. The stock market influences many aspects of people's lives, even people who own no **stock** and who live in places far away from Wall Street. Understanding the stock market gives you the power to understand changes in the economy that affect all of us.

Newspapers show tables with stock information laid out in rows and columns. At times, a table is more useful than a graph. You will use both tables and graphs to explore stocks in this lesson.

About Tables

When you look at a **table**, you will find labels at the top rather than at the bottom, as you do with graphs. Depending on the table, there might be labels on the left side too. In the table here, start by reading across the top. You might not understand all the labels at first. Take one or two that you do understand. Look at the third column labeled "Stock." Under this heading are the names of the companies. Can you find AC Moore? (*Hint*: The stocks are listed in alphabetical order.)

NASDAQ NATIONAL MARKET

52-Week High	52-Week Low	Stock	High	Low	Last	Chg
		A				
8.00	0.33	AConsul	0.45	0.36	0.36	–0.02
28.95	15.50	AAON	28.20	26.40	27.35	+0.85
26.38	4.56	AB Watl	7.93	6.50	7.60	+0.30
12.62	8.00	ABC Bop	12.10	11.19	12.00	+0.51
15.40	**5.75**	**AC Moore**	**15.50**	**14.00**	**15.50**	**+1.50**
10.50	0.69	ACE CO	1.67	1.44	1.52	–0.11

Here is how to read the statistics for the company ABC Bop.

52-Week High	The 52-week high is the highest price reached for a **share** of stock in the past year, not including the previous day. In the past year, the highest price for this stock at the close of the trading day was $12.62.
52-Week Low	In the past year, the lowest price for this stock at the end of the trading day was $8.00, not including the previous day.
Stock	The name of the company is ABC Bop.
High	At some point during the previous trading day, the high was $12.10. The high is the highest price for which the stock traded in regular trading (while the stock exchange was open) the previous day.
Low	At some point during the previous trading day, the low was $11.19. The low is the lowest price for which the stock traded in regular trading the previous day.
Last	The last price for a share of this stock at the end of the trading day was $12.00.
Chg	The change in the last price at the end of the previous trading day was +0.51 cents higher than what it had been the day before. Change is the difference between the last price the previous day and the last price two days before in regular trading.

Use your own words to explain AConsul's stock price on July 15, 2001.

Activity 1: Three Companies

For this activity, you will make your own tables of stock prices for three companies.

The graphs on the next two pages (Yahoo, Triton Energy, and Cisco Systems) represent each company's stock prices for a week. Tables are presented beside each graph.

Fill in the tables, starting with Day 1, Friday.

For each day, find the stock price and write both the name of the day and the stock price for that day in your table.

Pay attention to the labels on the *y*-axis!

You may have to estimate some prices since many of the points are between two *y*-axis labels.

1. Yahoo

Day	Price

Mean ______

Median ______

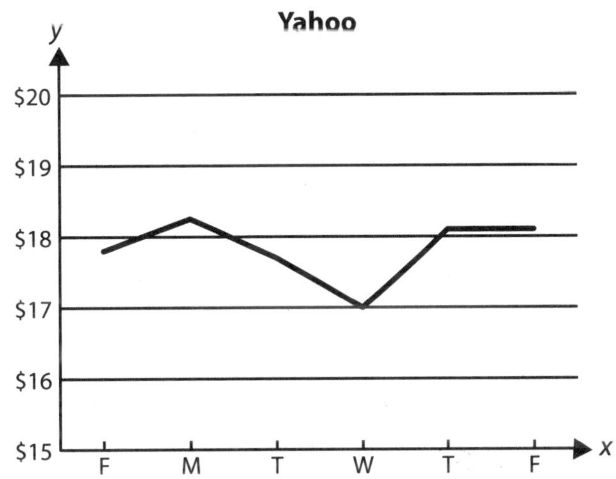

2. Triton Energy

Day	Price

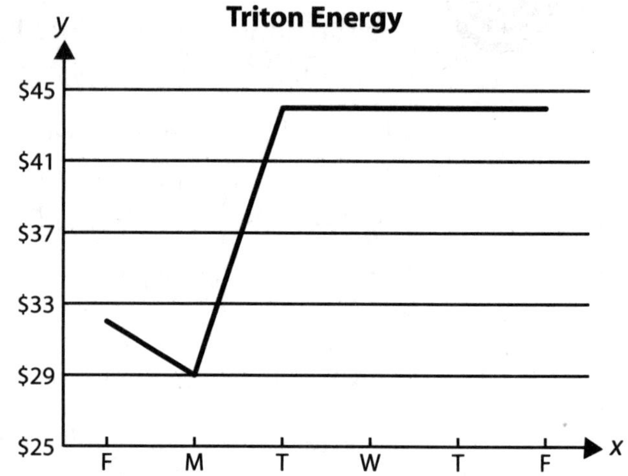

Mean ______

Median ______

3. Cisco Systems

Day	Price

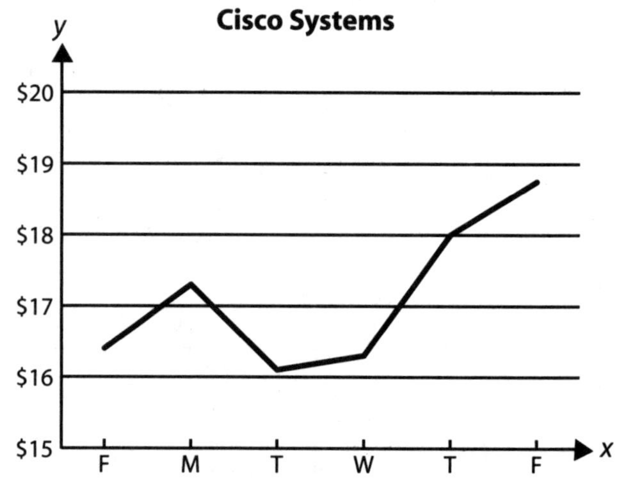

Mean ______

Median ______

Activity 2: Altering Scale

Use the information from the graph or table of Triton Energy stock price to sketch three new graphs. The scales will be different for each graph.

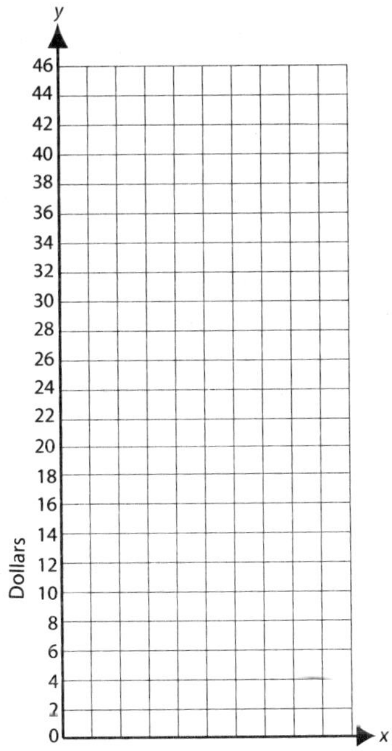

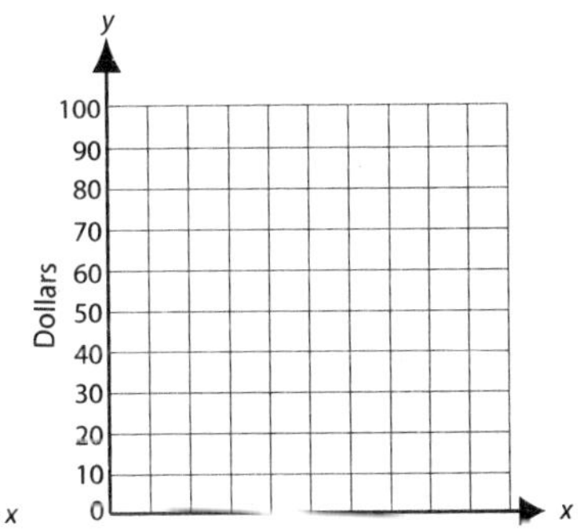

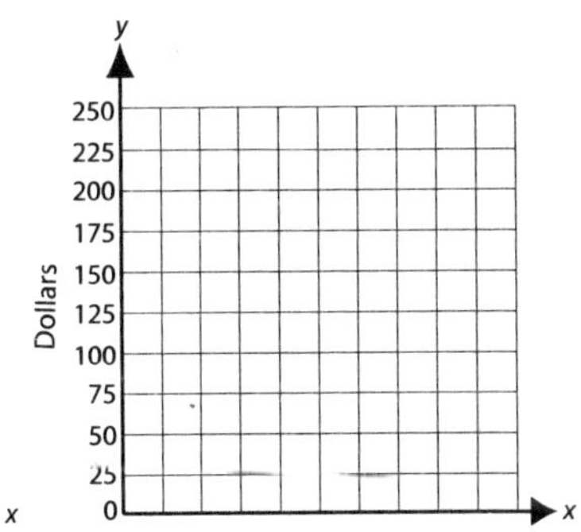

1. Before you start, predict which graph will have the steepest line: ____________

2. Predict which graph will have the flattest line: ____________

3. What do you notice about the different scales?

4. When the scale is $2.00, the line is…

5. When the scale is $10.00, the line is . . .

6. When the scale is $25.00, the line is . . .

7. The smaller the interval, the . . .

8. The larger the interval, the . . .

Practice: More Stocks—From Graphs to Tables

Use the information from the graphs to complete the tables.

Graph 1

Day	Price

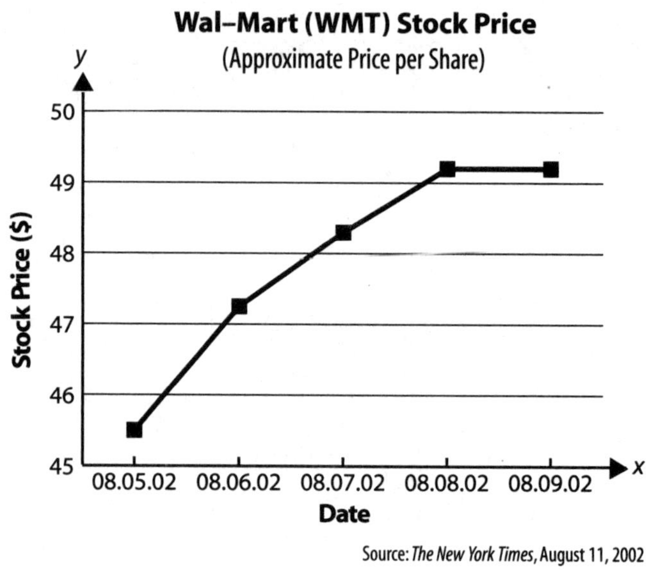

High for the week ______

Low for the week ______

Graph 2

Day	Price

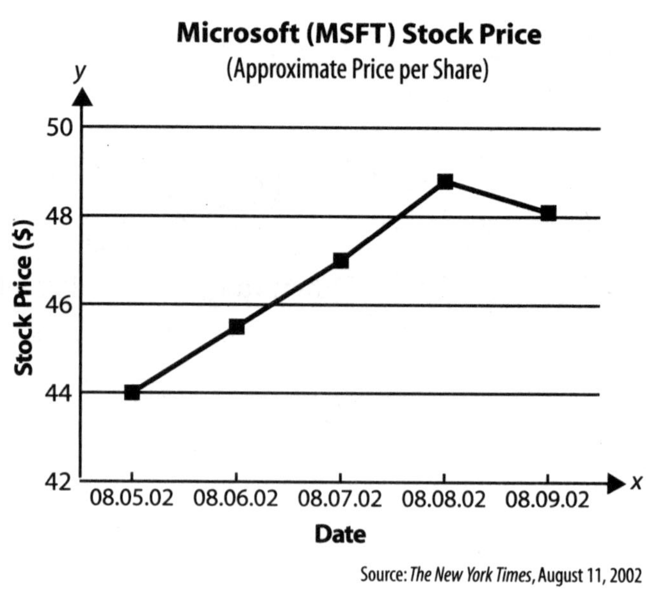

Opening price for the week ______

Closing price for the week ______

Graph 3

Day	Price

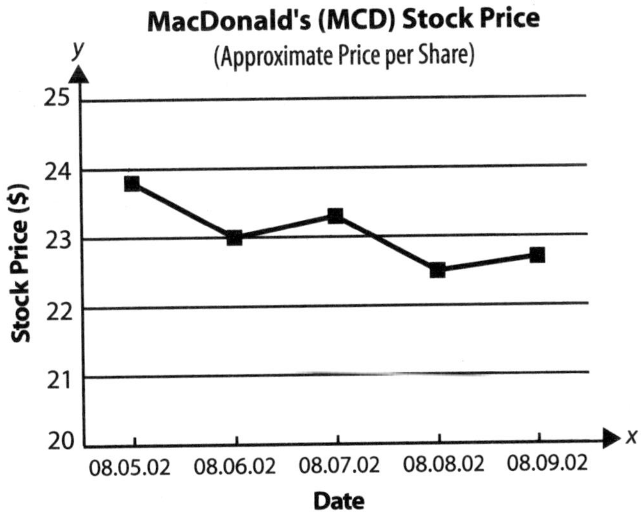

Source: *The New York Times*, August 11, 2002

Mean ______

Median ______

Practice: From Graphs to Stories—Stock Prices

The three graphs below show the stock prices of three companies over a five-day period in August 2002. Next to each graph, write a short description of what happened to the stock price of the company.

> Look back at your notes (especially vocabulary) for *Lesson 5*.
>
> Focus on what happened in the graph at the beginning, middle, and end.

Graph 1

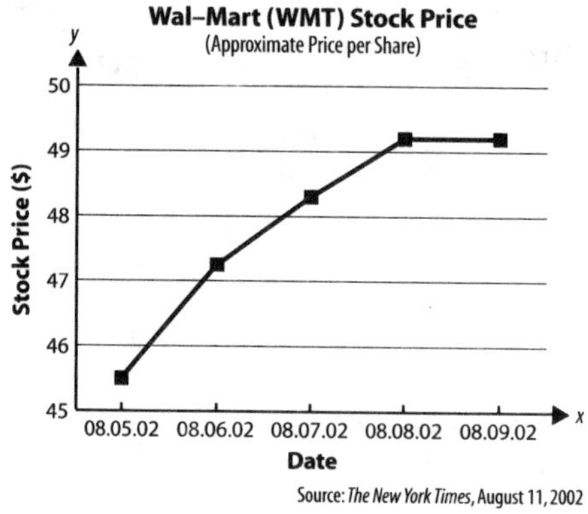

Story of the Graph

____

____

____

____

____

____

____

____

Graph 2

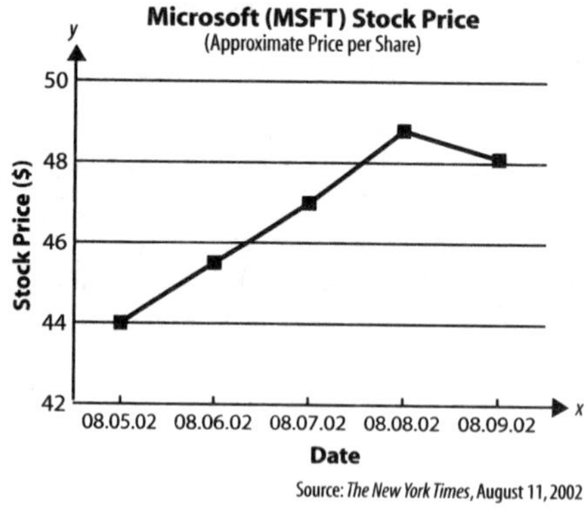

Story of the Graph

____

____

____

____

____

____

____

Graph 3

Story of the Graph

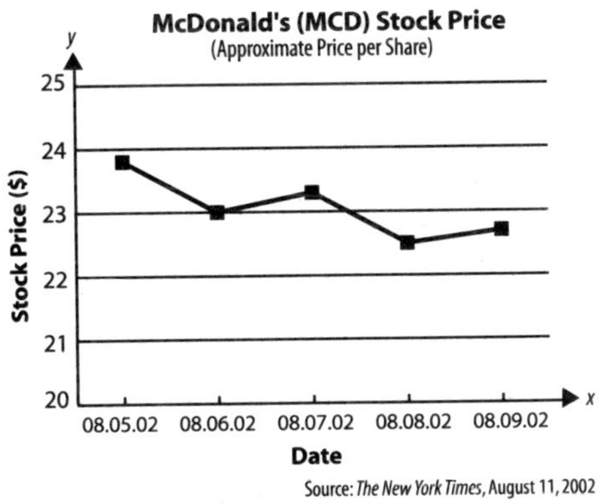

Based on the information in the three graphs, which company's stock would you consider buying?

Why?

Extension: What Is New with the Stock Market?

Most radio stations and newspapers report on some aspect of the stock market every day. Listen for the day's stock prices on the radio, or read about them in a newspaper. Then answer the questions.

1. What did you hear or read?

2. What questions do you have?

3. What do you think might happen next?

Test Practice

Items 1 and 2 refer to this graph.

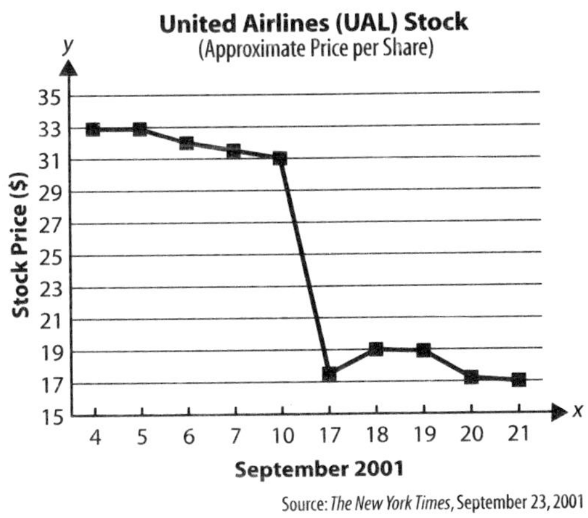

1. According to the graph, which of the following statements is *not* true?

   (1) The value of United Airlines (UAL) stock was dropping slowly before the week of September 10.

   (2) During the week of September 10, UAL stock fell to almost half of what it had been the previous week.

   (3) The UAL stock price for September 21 was lower than it was for September 17.

   (4) The UAL stock price for September 21 was almost half of what it was on September 4.

   (5) The price of UAL stock decreased by almost $2 between September 4 and September 10.

2. According to the graph, what conclusion can be drawn?

   (1) From September 17 on, the UAL stock price steadily increased.

   (2) UAL stock was on an upward trend before the week of September 10.

   (3) Stock prices almost doubled between September 17 and 18.

   (4) United Airlines was not able to rebound from the week of September 10.

   (5) UAL stock price held steady from September 17 on.

Problems 3–6 refer to the following graph. During

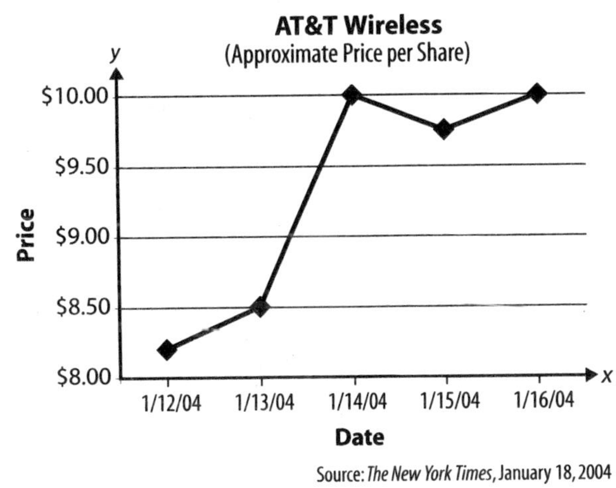

the week of January 12–16, 2004, there was a rumor that another company might buy the American Telephone & Telegraph (AT&T) Wireless Company.

3. On which day did the greatest change in the price of AT&T Wireless stock occur?

   (1) Monday, January 12

   (2) Tuesday, January 13

   (3) Wednesday, January 14

   (4) Thursday, January 15

   (5) Friday, January 16

4. What was the mean price for a share of AT&T Wireless stock for the week?

   (1) The same as the median price for that week

   (2) Less than the median price for that week

   (3) The same as the mode for that week

   (4) Higher than the median for the week

   (5) $10.00

5. Based on the graph and the story it tells, which of the following is true?

   (1) The stock increased, stayed the same, and then increased again.

   (2) The stock stayed the same, had a steep increase, and then stayed the same.

   (3) The stock increased steadily, decreased a little, and then increased again.

   (4) The stock decreased steadily.

   (5) The stock was constant, decreased, and then remained constant.

6. The median price for a share of AT&T Wireless stock for the week was ____________________.

STAGE | BROADWAY | SCREEN

VARIETY

PRICE 25¢

VOL. XCVII. No. 3 | NEW YORK, WEDNESDAY, OCTOBER 30, 1929 | 88 PAGES

WALL ST. LAYS AN EGG

Going Dumb Is Deadly to Hostess In Her Serious Dance Hall Profesh

DROP IN STOCKS ROPES SHOWMEN

Kidding Kissers in Talkers Burns Up Fans of Screen's Best Lovers

HOMELY WOMEN SCARCE; CAN'T EARN OVER $25

Closing the Unit: Stock Picks

Where would you put your money?

This lesson will give you another opportunity to explore the world of the stock market. You will use graphs of stock performance to compare companies. Then you will make a sales pitch to your classmates to invest in stock of a company you have chosen.

As you continue to develop confidence working with data and graphs, you will use them to make decisions, for example, figuring out the best investment. Skills you learn for analyzing data will likely save you money or time.

If you have access to the Internet, you can find graphs of stock prices. Try this:

- Go to http://www.nasdaq.com.

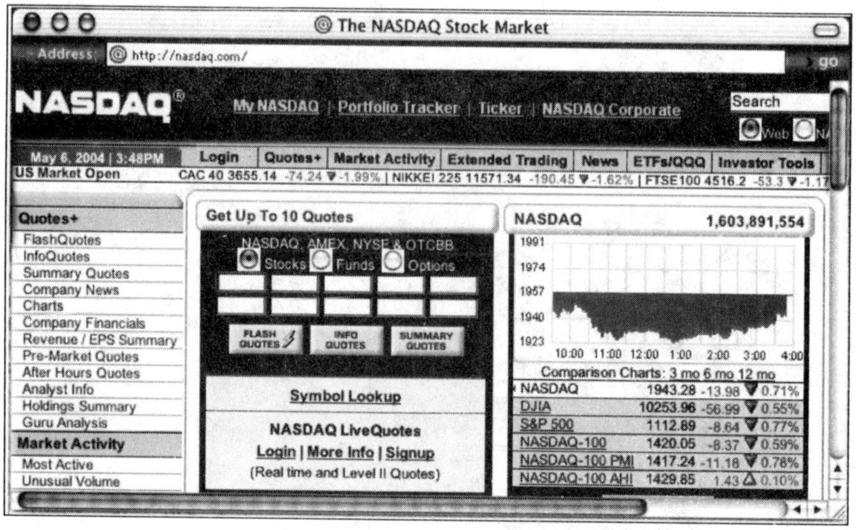

- Think of a company whose stock you would like to research.
- Find the symbol for that company. For example, "hnz" is the symbol for Heinz.
- Find the place on the site to create a chart.
- Select a five-year time frame and update the chart.
- To compare two stocks, find the symbol for the second company.
- Find the place on the site to compare stocks.
- Select a five-year time frame and update the chart. The graphs for both companies will appear in the chart.

Activity 1: Stock Picks

1. Which two companies are you comparing?

   Company 1

   Company 2

2. How would you describe the stock price for each company? Write your answers on a separate sheet of paper.

   a. How did each company begin?

   b. What happened in Year 2?

   c. What happened in Year 3?

   d. Which direction did the stock price take in Year 4?

   e. At the end of five years, where is the stock price compared to where it was at the end of Year 1? At the end of Year 4?

   f. What was the highest point? The lowest point?

   g. How do the highest and lowest points compare for the two companies?

3. Where did the greatest change (either up or down) occur in the five years?

4. Check the labels and scales.

Are your graphs using the same scales? If not, redo one so that the scales are the same, *or* put both lines on the same graph. How does that change your impression of the companies?

[Optional] Design a graph.

- Design a graph that shows off the stock of your choice. Choose one data point for each year. How could you change the scale to support your case for buying this stock?

- Design a graph that shows the stock you did *not* choose. (*Hint*: Make sure you choose a scale that demonstrates your point.)

Plan your opening and closing statements.

When you are ready to present to the class, think about your opening and closing statements. This is your chance to convince this audience to buy the stock. How can you win these people over right away? Think about which details you can point out to show you are informed and to build their confidence in you.

Activity 1: Stock Picks *(continued)*

Using two of the graphs, determine which company's stock you would purchase.

Pay attention to the y-axis amounts.

Be prepared to explain your reasoning.

1. HEINZ (HNZ)

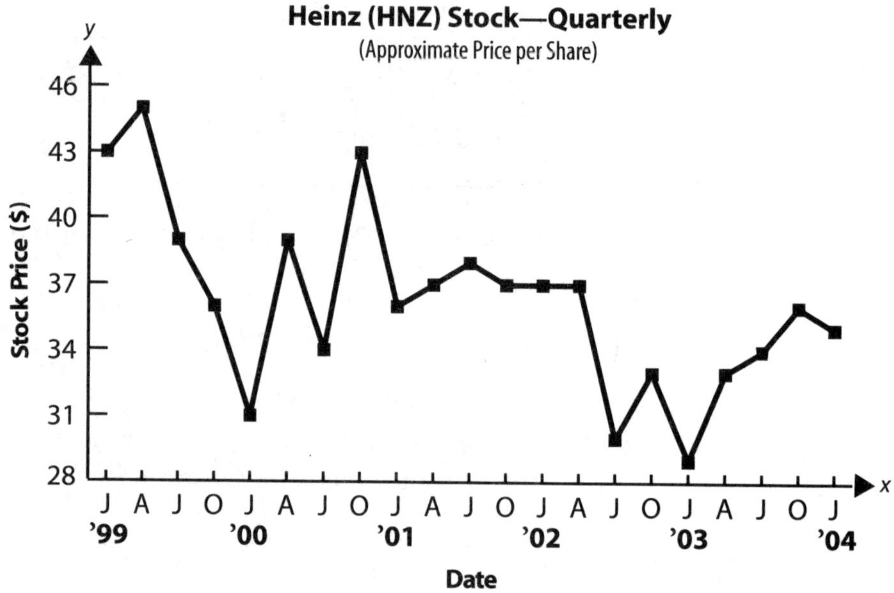

2. HERSHEY (HSY)

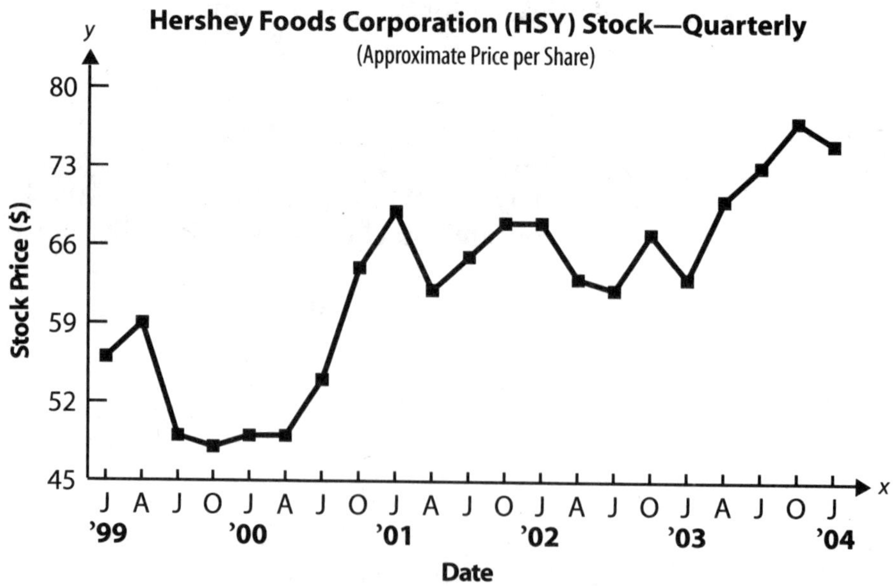

3. AVON (AVP)

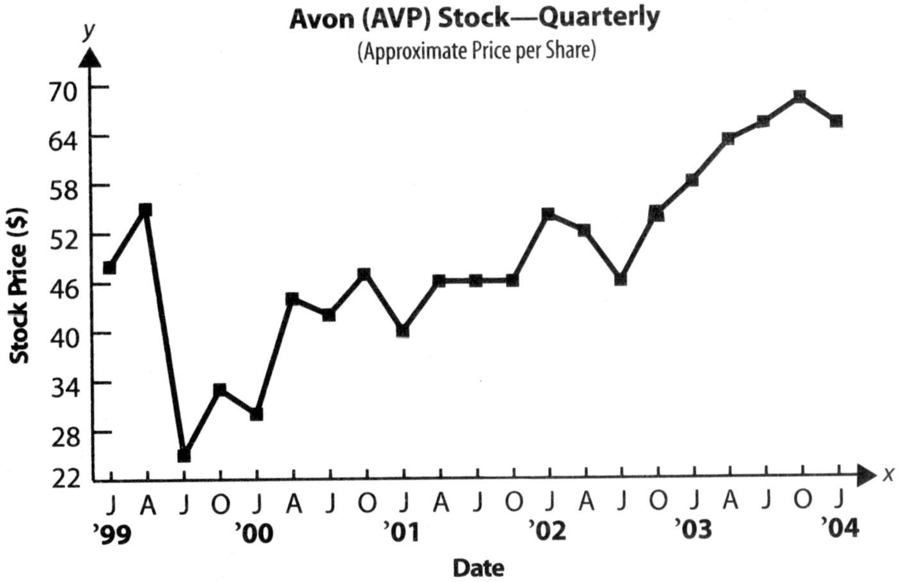

4. MARTHA STEWART (MSO)

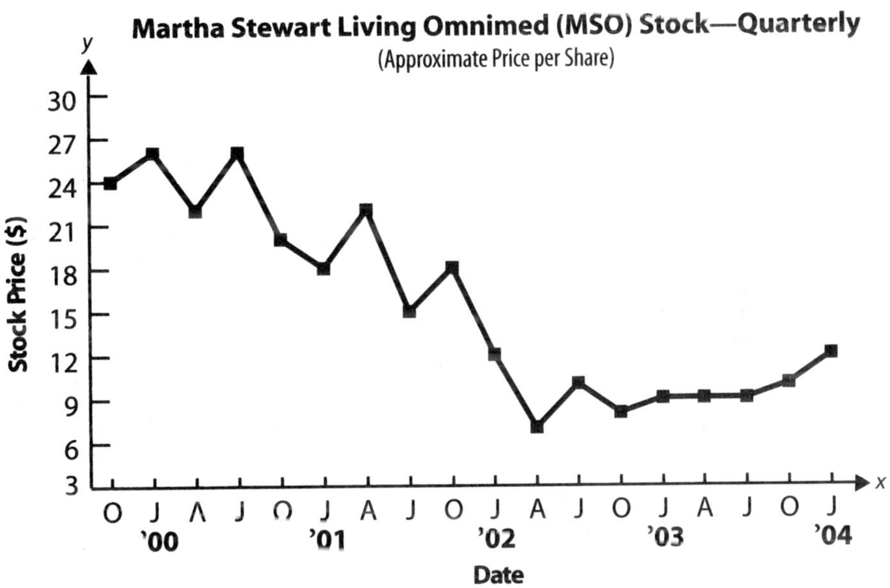

Activity 1: Stock Picks—Voting Sheet

Company Name				My Ranking

Activity 2: Review Session

Review what you learned in this unit.

- Go back to the practice pages in past lessons.
- Pick a page in each lesson.
- Cover up what you wrote on the page.
- Read the question only.
- Answer out loud or on paper.
- Reread your original answers to refresh your memory and check your work.

_____	Sort, group, and regroup data	*Lesson 1*
_____	Use fractions and percents to compare quantities on a graph	*Lessons 2* and *4*
_____	Make graphs	*Lessons 3* and *4*
_____	Tell the story of a graph	*Lessons 5* and *10*
_____	Plot points	*Lesson 6*
_____	Find mean, median, and mode	*Lessons 1*, *7*, and *9*
_____	Match a statement to a graph	*Lesson 8*

Making a portfolio of your best work will help you review the concepts and skills in this unit (see *Reflections* for *Closing the Unit: Stock Picks*, page 153, for ideas).

Activity 3: Final Assessment

Complete the tasks in the *Final Assessment.* When you finish, compare your first Mind Map, page 2, with your Mind Map from the *Final Assessment.*

What do you notice?

VOCABULARY

Lesson	Terms, Symbols, Concepts	Definitions and Examples
Opening the Unit	criteria	
	horizontal	
	vertical	
	graph	
1	data	
	frequency graph	
	mode	
	category	
2	sample	
	audience	
	benchmark	
3	bar graph	
	circle graph	
	vertical or y-axis	
	horizontal or x-axis	

VOCABULARY *(continued)*

LESSON	TERMS, SYMBOLS, CONCEPTS	DEFINITIONS AND EXAMPLES
4	benchmark percents	
	benchmark fractions	
	100%	
5	line graph	
	increase/decrease	
6	change over time	
	trends	
	scale	
7	average	
	mean	
	outlier	
8	climate graph	
	precipitation	

VOCABULARY *(continued)*

LESSON	TERMS, SYMBOLS, CONCEPTS	DEFINITIONS AND EXAMPLES
9	median	
10	stocks	
	shares	
	stock market	
	approximate	
	table	

REFLECTIONS

OPENING THE UNIT: Many Points Make a Point

What did you learn by sorting graphs?

When do you see and use graphs in your life?

LESSON 1: Countries in Our Closets

What does a person need to pay attention to when organizing data?

A student once said, "When we change the categories, we keep losing information." Give an example of what she meant.

What are the three components of a frequency graph?

LESSON 2: Most of Us Eat . . .

What does a person need to pay attention to when organizing data?

Which skills do you want to improve (for example, organizing, categorizing, or making statements about data)?

LESSON 3: Displaying Data in a New Way

List what you know about bar graphs and circle graphs.

What do you still wonder about?

LESSON 4: A Closer Look at Circle Graphs

What do you know now about circle graphs that you did not know before?

What are important questions to ask when looking at circle graphs?

MIDPOINT ASSESSMENT

What do you know now that you did not know before starting the unit, *Many Points Make a Point*?

LESSON 5: Sketch This

What do you want to remember about how line graphs tell a story?

LESSON 6: Roller-Coaster Rides

Make a list titled "What I practiced today."

When are some times you might see and use information from a line graph? Who do you know who could talk to you about line graphs?

LESSON 7: A Mean Idea

List some ways to find the mean.

What words will help you remember the idea of mean?

When would you use a mean?

LESSON 8: Mystery Cities

What do you want to remember about graphs that show two kinds of information?

List the skills you have learned in math class that helped you read climate graphs.

LESSON 9: Median

What are three main points to remember about the median?

How is the median different from the mean?

How is the median different from the mode?

LESSON 10: Stock Prices

What new information did you learn about the stock market?

What are you curious about?

CLOSING THE UNIT: Stock Picks

Your Best Work

Review work you have done in class and on your own. Pick out two assignments you think are your best work or show where you learned the most.

Make a cover sheet that includes

- Your name
- Date
- Names of the assignments

For each assignment that you pick,

- Write a sentence or two describing the piece of work.
- Write a sentence or two explaining what skills were required to complete the work.
- Write a sentence or two explaining why you picked this piece of work.

Take some time to look through your work.

What did you do?

What did you learn?

Look back at your *Reflections* and *Vocabulary* to get more ideas.

SPREADSHEET GUIDE USING MICROSOFT® EXCEL

There are many spreadsheet programs available with which you can create graphs and charts. The following guide is based on a Microsoft Excel spreadsheet.

1. Organize the data that you want to enter into the spreadsheet.
2. Open a new Excel document—a Workbook. You will see a grid with boxes. Each box is called a cell. Type your name in cell A1 and today's date in cell A2. Save your file and give it a name, like "Sporting Event Attendance."
3. Type the labels, going across rows or down columns—for example, months, years, ice cream flavors, sports. Type the numbers for each category in the cell next to or underneath that category.

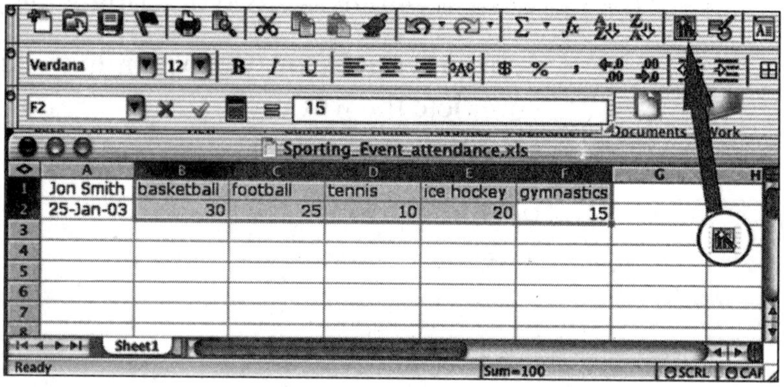

4. Once you have entered all the data, highlight the data (including the column titles), and click the Chart Wizard icon.
5. Choose "Pie" as the type of chart. Click "Next."

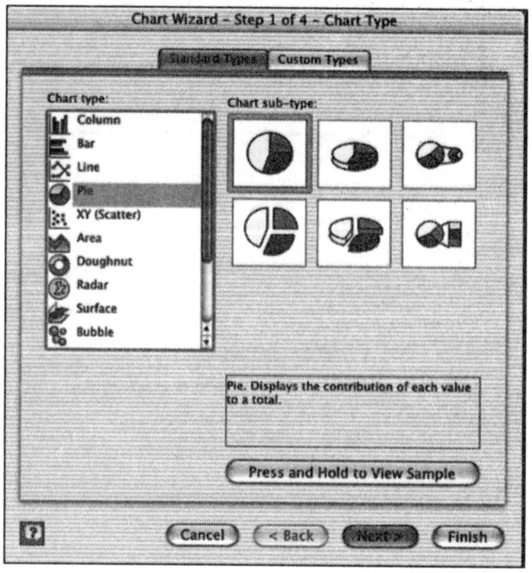

6. The next window says "Review the data range"; if you have highlighted everything you want graphed, click "Next."
7. Give the chart a title ("Sporting Event Attendance," for example). Click "Next."
8. To paste the chart onto the spreadsheet, click "Finish."

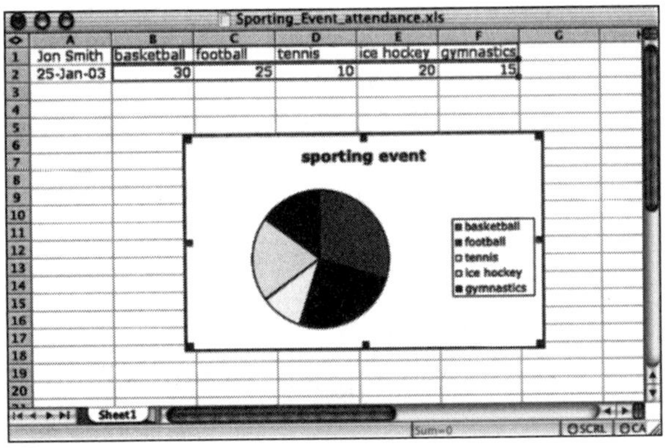

9. If you want the circle graph to show percents, double-click on the pie chart. It will say "Format Data Series." Click on "Data Labels." Then click on "Show Percent." Click "OK." Your circle graph will now show percents.
10. If you want a bar graph instead, follow the same directions, but choose "Bar" instead of "Pie," and continue.

Adapted and reprinted with permission of Pat Fina
Community Learning Center, Cambridge, MA

SOURCES AND RESOURCES

Health

For facts about blood and blood banks, see the American Association of Blood Banks, http://www.aabb.org.

For HIV/AIDS data, see http://www.aidshotline.org/crm/asp/refer/statistics.

For data on homicides and suicides, see the Centers for Disease Control and Prevention, http://www.cdc.gov.

For prescription medication costs, see http://bernie.house.gov/prescriptions/drugsheet.asp.

Immigration

For the Department of Homeland Security, see http://uscis.gov.

For the United Nations High Commission on Refugees, see http://www.unhcr.ch.

Parks, Land, Recreation

"Change in Land Use, 1985–1999." *Mass Audubon Losing Ground: At What Cost?* Reprinted with permission from the Massachusetts Audubon Society, 2003.

Attendance data on amusement parks reprinted with permission from the International Association of Amusement Parks and Attractions, http://www.iaapa.org.

"Ups and Downs at the Park" reprinted with permission from the *Boston Herald*, June 4, 2000.

For data on National Park Service visitors, see http://www2.nature.nps.gov/stats.

Stocks

NASDAQ home page reprinted with permission from NASDAQ Stock Market, Inc.

Tyson, Eric. *Investing for Dummies*, 2nd edition. New York: Wiley Publishing, 1999.

Transportation

For commuting times, see the Census Bureau, http://www.census.gov.

"Countries with the Greatest Number of Elevators," "Elevators per 10,000 Population for the Above Countries," and "Elevator Traffic" reprinted with permission from the National Building Museum. For more information, see the exhibit catalog: *Up, Down, Across: Elevators, Escalators, and Moving Sidewalks*, London: Merrell Publishers, 2003.

Work

For data on inflation, employment, wages, and safety, see the Department of Labor, http://stats.bls.gov.

For data on clothing manufacturing, see http://www.globalexchange.org/campaigns/sweatshops.

"Changing Needs of the American Workforce" reprinted with permission of the Association for Career and Technical Education, http://www.acteonline.org.

Other

For lots of fun facts, see http://www.infoplease.com or http://www.factmonster.com.

Make your own graphs on http://nces.ed.gov/nceskids/graphing. The site has an easy-to-read interface.

For interesting data on crime trends and graphs with matching statements, see the Department of Justice, Bureau of Justice, Statistics, http://www.ojp.usdoj.gov/bjs/glance.htm.

"Going Wireless" graphs reprinted with permission from the Chicago Tribune Company, 2000.

Spreadsheet Guide screenshots reprinted by permission from Microsoft® Corporation. Microsoft Excel X for Mac © 1985–2001, Microsoft Corporation. All rights reserved.

"Spreadsheet Guide Using Microsoft® Excel" adapted and reprinted with permission of Pat Fina, Community Learning Center, Cambridge, MA.

McGee, Lynn. "Where Are Our Clothes Made? Field Testing the EMPower Curriculum." *The Math Exchange* (Spring 2002): 8–12.

Zawojewski, J. S., and J. Michael Shaughnessy. "Mean and Median: Are They Really So Easy?" *Mathematics Teaching in the Middle School* 5 (March 2000): 436–40.

For interactive Java applets for students or teachers, see http://www.shodor.org.

For math questions, see "Have a math question? Ask Dr. Math!" http://mathforum.org/dr.math.